MANY ARE CALLED

MANY ARE CALLED

*Rediscovering the Glory
of the Priesthood*

SCOTT HAHN

DOUBLEDAY

New York · London · Toronto · Sydney · Auckland

⫢D
DOUBLEDAY

Published in the United States by Doubleday Religion,

an imprint of the Crown Publishing Group,

a division of Random House, Inc., New York.

www.crownpublishers.com

DOUBLEDAY is a registered trademark and the DD colophon is a trademark of

Random House, Inc.

All scriptural quotations are from the Revised Standard Version

of the Bible, Catholic Edition.

Library of Congress Cataloging-in-Publication Data

Hahn, Scott.

Many are called : rediscovering the glory of the priesthood / Scott Hahn.—1st ed.

1. Vocation, Ecclesiastical. 2. Priesthood—Catholic Church. I. Title.

BX2380.H34 2010

253'.2—dc22   2009051598

ISBN 978-0-307-59077-0

PRINTED IN THE UNITED STATES OF AMERICA

10   9   8   7   6   5   4   3   2   1

First Edition

For Monsignor George Yontz, pastor, father, and friend,

in gratitude for a life of priestly service

and your dedication to changing our lives for the better

CONTENTS

CONTENTS

FOREWORD

By Archbishop Timothy Dolan

E VER SINCE I was a boy, I recognized there was something unique about priests. I knew that they had great responsibilities. I saw that they were always there for the most important moments in life—baptisms, weddings, funerals, or the side of sickbeds. I figured they were special because they were Jesus' men, men who radiated joy in the service of the Church, men set apart for the things of God. I knew that their lives weren't easy; neither was Jesus'. Yet I also knew that their sacrifices were the stuff that made life worth living, just like Jesus'. And from early on, I wanted to be one.

I thank the Lord daily for the Church, for the People of God, and especially for men like Dr. Scott Hahn. In *Many Are Called: Rediscovering the Glory of the Priesthood,* Scott speaks profoundly about the priesthood. His insights are compelling. As a former Presbyterian minister, now a Catholic theologian, and as a loving husband and the father of six children, Scott looks upon priests from a matchless vantage point. He says, "When men really know what the priesthood is, they are instinctively attracted to it. It is instinctively attractive." One of the strong points of *Many Are Called* is Scott's explanation of the priesthood as a call of Christ to men who come to serve as fathers, protectors, and providers for the People of God.

Throughout the pages of *Many Are Called,* Scott traces some of the story lines of the history of salvation, plumbs the depths of Sacred Scripture, and outlines God's plan for the priesthood. For example, he speaks of Adam and Abram as priestly prototypes, the former in his fatherhood of humanity and the latter in terms of his mediation for Sodom; likewise, he reminds us of how priests and mediators like Peter and Paul exercised the role of fatherhood as God's coworkers. Just as men often are identified by their trades, identified as who they are by what they do, so Scott shows how priests strive to imitate the Word they preach. Each priest is another Christ.

"As Church and as priests," said Pope Benedict XVI, when inaugurating June 2009 to June 2010 as the Year for Priests, "we proclaim Jesus of Nazareth Lord and Christ, Crucified and Risen, Sovereign of time and of history, in the glad certainty that this truth coincides with the deepest expectations of the human heart." The human heart is, indeed, only satisfied with Christ. As Saint Augustine reminds us in his *Confessions,* our hearts will ever be restless until they rest in God. Scott, one of our foremost Catholic theologians, helps us to see the priest's role in mediating God's peace to his people.

In this Year for Priests, each of us has an exceptional opportunity to reflect upon the priesthood. It is my fervent prayer that this Year for Priests will bear much fruit: an increase in vocations to the priesthood, a renewal among priests of their own identity, a sense of gratitude among God's people for the priesthood, and a more profound devotion to Christ the High Priest. It is with a sense of awe and gratitude that I shall reflect not only on my boyhood experiences, but also on my own thirty-three years of priesthood. I invite you, as you read *Many Are Called,* to join with me in rediscovering the glory of the priesthood.

+ *Timothy M. Dolan*
Archbishop of New York
November 30, 2009
Year for Priests

MANY ARE CALLED

1

Measures of Manhood

Not Your Average Joe

JOE FREEDY enjoyed the kind of life my friends and I envied when we were teens. He was starting quarterback for the State University of New York at Buffalo. The Bulls are an NCAA Division I team, so his games were broadcast worldwide on ESPN and other sports networks. As a senior, he finished fourth in his conference in passing yards. Two of the men ahead of him, Ben Roethlisberger and Byron Leftwich, would go on to be superstars in the National Football League. He was on the "must invite" list for the best parties on campus, and with his linebacker roommate he went from one to the next. He had movie-star good looks—even when he wasn't wearing his helmet and face mask—and most of the university's thousands of young women knew who he was.

My buddies and I dreamed of such a life, with sports to gratify our competitive urges, television cameras to feed our egos, beautiful girls to confirm our sex appeal—and the promise of prodigious earning power, from a professional contract and endorsements. For us, that all added up to fulfillment. It marked a certain pinnacle of manhood.

Joe Freedy was Catholic, one of five children raised by devout parents, but God was second-string in his life and spent most of the time forgotten on the sidelines. Joe later recalled for a reporter: "I was into football and image. I'd put in an hour Sunday and as soon as I hit the parking lot I forgot about God until next Sunday."

Football and image remained his preoccupations. What else was there? Old Milwaukee used to advertise its beer with scenes from the sporting and partying life. They ran with the tag line: "It doesn't get any better than this." Maybe that's what Joe Freedy believed.

Gridiron and Grace

Then his father loaned him a book about the Mass. Joe started reading and found he couldn't stop. The book presented the Mass in terms that were unfamiliar to him.

Drawing from the vision of John in the Book of Revelation, the author spoke of the Mass as "heaven on earth" and drew out the implications of the Catholic doctrine of the Real Presence. Jesus is truly present in the Eucharist—body, blood, soul, and divinity—and this is the fulfillment of certain promises he made during his earthly ministry. "I am the living bread which came down from heaven; if any one eats of this bread, he will live for ever; and the bread which I shall give for the life of the world is my flesh" (Jn 6:51). "And he took bread, and when he had given thanks he broke it and gave it to them, saying, 'This is my body which is given for you'" (Lk 22:19). "I am with you always, to the close of the age" (Mt 28:20).

As Joe read on, he learned that when the priest speaks the words of institution, "This is my body," Christ is present, attended by all the angels and the saints. He comes in glory—all the glory that he has possessed since the beginning of time, all the glory he will have at the end of time. And this presence is the very definition of heaven. It is a foretaste, because we cannot yet see him in his glory. It is, however, no less real and no less glorious.

These truths upended Joe and revolutionized his experience of going to Church. Here's the way he explained it: "If someone never watched football and went to a game without knowing the rules and the strategies, they probably wouldn't enjoy it. When I learned what was happening at the Mass . . . I enjoyed it more."

Joe started going to Mass more often, and then every day. His teammates noticed a big change right away. Joe was still Joe, but he had matured, grown more serious about life. He wasn't interested in partying.

The new experience woke him up to something more. Now listening more closely in prayer, Joe soon discerned God's call. God was calling him to the priesthood.

He went on with the season and finished very well, ending up third in career passing yards at Buffalo, whose football program stretched back more than a hundred years.

In spring of 2002, he graduated with a bachelor's degree in communications; three months later, he began studies at St. Paul Seminary in Pittsburgh, a demanding six-year program in preparation for his ordination. He went on to score two graduate degrees, one from a Roman university, and in his spare time complete Spanish-language studies in Mexico.

On the morning of Saturday, June 21, 2008, Bishop David Zubik ordained Joseph Freedy to the priesthood of Jesus Christ. It was more than a new game, more than a new season, more than a new team, even more than a new career. For Father Joe it was a new life, a new way of being. (More on that later.)

Within a year he found himself serving as a chaplain for the Missionaries of Charity, the religious order founded by Blessed Mother Teresa of Calcutta. They, in turn, inspired him to spend his Christmas break in 2008 in Ethiopia, among the poorest of the poor. Once back in Pittsburgh, he soon made the news when he was among the first clergymen to show up at the scene when a mass murder had taken place at a suburban fitness club.

Many are called to the priesthood. Not every man who answers the call comes with a story like Joe's—though they all come with a story—but they all receive what Father Joe received. They receive the priesthood of Christ and the divine power to bring his sacraments to a world that needs them.

Every priest gets what Father Joe got. Ultimately, they get a supernatural fulfillment of something God gave them by nature: manhood, masculinity. That's why we address them as "Father."

Manhood, fatherhood . . . it doesn't get any better than this.

Masculinity and Its Counterfeits

The television commercials, however, tell a different story, don't they? All the popular media, in fact, draw from certain stereotypes when they want to convey masculinity. Instead of the real deal, they give us machismo, which is a caricature of masculinity.

They show us men who are sexually promiscuous, physically aggressive, and ostentatiously wealthy. They would have us believe that the measure of manhood is to be found in a guy's bedroom and backseat exploits, his fistfights (sublimated, perhaps, into competitive sports), or his prodigal spending.

The stereotypes would have us believe that the Y chromosome—maleness—will remain unfulfilled as long as any of these things is lacking. My friends and I believed this when we were teenagers, though I don't think we could have articulated it. Our male role models were professional athletes, rock stars, and young, successful entrepreneurs who lived large. We would have been baffled by quarterback Joe Freedy's vocational decision as well as Father Joe Freedy's sense of fulfillment.

Please don't get me wrong. I have nothing against professional sports, rock music, or the free market. I'm an avid fan of all three. I don't believe the media, however, give us the best images of men in these fields. The cameraman gravitates toward the wide receiver who does an elaborate dance in the end zone. The reporter rushes to the boxer who will make the most outrageous claims. Paparazzi chase a stoned singer-songwriter through Southern California just to get a snapshot of him with his mistress. Why? Because provocative movement makes for "good" TV. Scandal makes for "good" newspaper copy.

Again, I'm not bashing the sport or the music. For every steroid- or cocaine-fueled prima donna out there, there's someone like Lou Gehrig, the Yankees first baseman, who quietly and courageously shows up for thousands of games, even when he's injured—who tips generously but not in a showy way, and who takes good care of his mother. There's a Roberto Clemente, the Pirates outfielder, who risked his life at the peak of his career, and lost it, trying to help the victims of a natural disaster in a faraway land.

Nevertheless, we have to admit that the stereotypes dominate the media and dominate the consciousness of young males (and many not-so-young males). When a young Joe Freedy said that his whole life was "football and image," the image he had in mind was surely that of the "guy's guy," which he picked up from the halftime beer commercials. In time, he learned that machismo does not satisfy, does not fulfill, a man—and he learned of something that does.

The Hidden Truth About Men

Why do so many men seek fulfillment and satisfaction where it cannot be found? Why do we settle for counterfeits rather than the real thing? Why do we believe the media's distortions of masculinity?

We believe them precisely *because* they are counterfeits, caricatures, and stereotypes. All such falsehoods depend upon a basis of truth, which they oversimplify, distort, or exaggerate.

When the media portray men as libidinous, aggressive, and greedy, they're grossly distorting authentic male roles—*fatherly* roles— namely, *life-giver, protector,* and *provider.* In the normal course of family life, a father is progenitor; he gives life, through the sexual expression of his love for his wife. In the normal course of family life, a father is the one who *defends* the family from outside threats; in extreme cases that can involve a violent intervention. In the normal course of family life, a father *provides* for his wife and children, as wage-earner and breadwinner, but also as a wise counselor, patient teacher, and steady emotional support.

What happens when these roles are severed from one another, severed from fatherhood, and deprived of their religious meaning, which is deeply theological?

When that happens, we encounter men in society as we find them in the media.

When it happens to us personally, we feel continually frustrated, confused, dissatisfied, unfulfilled.

What I hope to do in the course of this book is to recover the biblical and theological truth about priesthood and fatherhood. Here's why: Those two realities are profoundly related to each other. What's more, those terms describe the roles for which men—*males*—were created. God made men to be fathers. He called men to be fathers. And our hearts are restless till we rest in the role for which we were created, body and soul, and for which we were called by God and his Church.

I am a happily married man, proud father to five sons and a daughter and grandfather of three. I thank God for the fatherhood he has conferred upon me. Yet I believe that he has conferred a more perfect, and ultimately more fulfilling, fatherhood on Joe Freedy and those he has called to the priesthood.

Freed Up for Service

But I'm getting ahead of myself. That's the truth I want to work out in the rest of this book. It's a truth that God has revealed from the beginning of creation, in nature and in Scripture. In the chapters that follow, we'll trace the story line of "salvation history," highlighting the development of fatherhood and priesthood as God's people try, sometimes succeeding and sometimes failing, to live out those roles.

If we understand fatherhood and priesthood from God's point of view, we'll be better equipped to help men discern their vocation and live it out faithfully. For *many* are called. In fact, *all* men have a vocation to fatherhood of one sort or another. But many are called to the fatherhood of priesthood.

What is priesthood? The answer to that question is spread throughout the Bible, but distilled in the teaching of the Church. We'll review the basic Catholic teaching before we explore its strong foundations in Scripture.

Remember the book that changed Joe Freedy's outlook on worship and changed the course of his life? Well, it's my prayer that this little book might do for the priesthood what that book did for the Mass, at least in the case of one quarterback in Buffalo, New York. It's not just vanity that makes me hope so. I speak from experience. I've written a few books, and I know that writing is hard work for the author.

Reading, though—when it's done right—can be a collaboration between the reader and the Holy Spirit; and that's when reading a book is a far greater work than writing one. If at least a few readers call upon the help of the Spirit when they read these pages, then my prayer will be answered.

2

The Priest Common Denominator

A Review of the Basics

I GREW UP PRESBYTERIAN, but in a neighborhood
with many Catholic families. I noticed, early in life,
that my Catholic friends were different in many ways
from me and my Protestant friends. Take geography. We
tended to mark municipal boundaries according to school
district: *Do you go to Mount Lebanon or Bethel Park?* Just
cross a street and you went to a different junior high. You
might as well be in a different country.

Catholics, though, divided the lands up by parish. *Do you
belong to St. Bernard's or St. Germaine's?* And then there was
a further step in Catholic geography. Each parish was identified with its pastor: Father Lonergan at St. Bernard's,

Father Hugo at St. Germaine's. I'm somewhat amazed that I, who grew up Presbyterian, can remember such details after all these years. For mainstream geography, at school, I had to memorize the capitals of the major nations of the world, and I probably couldn't name half of them for you today. Yet I still remember the parishes and their pastors, whom I never met. No matter: Nations and capitals have come and gone, but the parishes are still in place, and the parishioners still revere the memory of those pastors.

Catholics know who their priests are. That's for sure. Are we as clear about *what a priest is*? Maybe not.

It's Not Just a Job

If I had asked my old friends in the neighborhood, they probably would have told me that a priest is to a Catholic parish what a minister is to a Protestant church. He's the overall manager of the operation, and he leads the worship every Sunday.

There is some truth to that. The "job" of a priest, as it unfolds in the course of an ordinary week, can bear many surface similarities to the "job" of a Protestant minister—a position I myself held for a time before my conversion to Catholicism. As a Presbyterian pastor, I preached sermons. I counseled people. I visited the sick. I worried about the church's leaky roof. I worked with the congregation's "session of elders" and took part in fund-raising programs. I held all those duties in common with the Catholic clergy at the parish across town.

There were, however, vast and deep differences between us Protestant ministers and those Catholic priests. For there are vast and deep differences in the way Catholic priests and Protestant ministers understand their office, their work, and their lives.

The Protestant ministry arose out of the sixteenth-century Protestant Reformation, and it was conceived as a conscious rejection of the traditional Catholic understanding of the priesthood. Thus, the differences are very important. They were important enough to cause long-standing divisions among Christians. I'm not writing this to dwell on the differences, but we should be aware of them, because they do affect the way we think of our clergy. This is especially true for those of us who live in societies whose histories have been shaped by Protestant Christianity.

We'll come back to those differences in a moment. For now it's enough for us to examine what the Catholic Church teaches about the priesthood.

For the Sake of the Sacraments

From the start I should make clear that priests are indeed *ministers*. They are ordained for ministry. The word *ministry* means "service," and ministers are servants. The Church's catechism makes clear that a priest's life is "at the service of" his congregation. The remainder of his lifetime after ordination is "a term of service." What he does in his ministry "must therefore be measured against the model of Christ, who by love made himself the least and the servant of all. The Lord said clearly that concern for his flock was proof of love for him."

Now, there are many ways a man can serve the people of his community. He can mow their lawns, prepare their taxes, cater their wedding receptions, or change the oil in their cars, and these are all noble endeavors. They are not, however, the ways a priest is called to serve.

The New Testament is quite specific about the primary duties and ministry of priests. They are ritual and sacrificial, as we read in the Letter to the Hebrews: "For every high priest chosen from among men is appointed to act on behalf of men in relation to God, to offer gifts and sacrifices for sins" (Heb 5:1). What can we draw from this? A priest is someone who offers sacrifice. A priest is someone who mediates between God and mankind. That is the nature of his service.

When Jesus commissioned his apostles (collectively) for specific works, these works were invariably sacramental and ritual. We see this in every single one of the Gospels. Jesus commanded the apostles to baptize: "Go therefore and make disciples of all nations, baptizing them" (Mt 28:19). He told them to say Mass: "He took bread, and . . . broke it . . . saying, 'This is my body . . . Do this in remembrance of me'" (Lk 22:19). He empowered them to hear confessions and absolve sinners: "If you forgive the sins of any, they are forgiven; if you retain the sins of any, they are retained" (Jn 20:23). He sent them out to anoint the sick: "And he called to him the twelve, and began to send them out . . . And they . . . anointed with oil many that were sick" (Mk 6:7, 13).

Thus, then as now, the primary work of the priest is liturgical and sacramental. A priest may do counseling, management, fund-raising, and so on, but that work is incidental to his life. He was ordained for the sake of sacramental ministry.

That was the case in Jesus' day, and it has been so ever since. This understanding of ministry, however, was hardly new by the time of the New Covenant. In both Hebrew and Greek, the same word is used to describe both ritual worship and manual labor. The word can be rendered as *service*—servile labor—or as *liturgy.* Even today, we refer to our acts of ritual public worship as both "services" and "liturgies."

By Any Other Name

This sacramental dimension is what makes Catholic ministry "priestly." When the biblical authors spoke of the "ministers" of the tabernacle or Temple, they used a specific word to describe them. In Greek it was *hiereus,* meaning, literally, "sacred person." That's the word we usually translate into English as "priest." The title didn't mean that those men were particularly wise, kind, or righteous. It meant simply that they were set apart for holy service. Their work was holy because God had ordained it, not because of any intrinsic worthiness of the priest.

So, in the Old Testament and the New, the terms *priest* and *minister* are used somewhat interchangeably. The priests fulfilled a sacrificial ministry, a service to the whole community. St. Paul understood his role in priestly terms. He spoke of his calling as "the grace given me by God to be a minister of Christ Jesus to the Gentiles in the priestly service of the gospel of God" (Rom 15:15–16).

With the coming of Christ, there was a "change in the

priesthood" (Heb 7:12). Jesus himself was now the high priest of the New Covenant. In fact, St. Paul spoke of Jesus as both sacrificial priest and sacrificial victim (see Eph 5:2).

But Jesus also shared his priesthood with men he designated as apostles; he commanded them to observe the rites he established, the sacraments of the Church, the sacraments of the New Covenant. As a priest of Christ, St. Paul could claim the rights formerly extended only to the priesthood of the Jerusalem Temple. "Do you not know that those who are employed in the temple service get their food from the temple, and those who serve at the altar share in the sacrificial offerings? In the same way, the Lord commanded that those who proclaim the gospel should get their living by the gospel" (1 Cor 9:13–14).

The English word *priest* itself comes from yet another New Testament word, the Greek *presbuteros* (which the Latins elided as *prester*). The word appears often in the New Testament, and it is usually translated as "elder." In the Epistle of St. James (5:14), for example, it describes the men—no doubt drawn from the more mature Christians—who received the call to sacramental ministry. There we see them anointing the sick and forgiving sins.

What Makes a Priest?

Unlike the priests of the Old Covenant, the priesthood of Jesus Christ did not fall to men by inheritance or fleshly descent. It came by vocation. Christ looked men in the eye and called them out: "Follow me" (see, for example, Mt 4:19 and 9:9). From then on, they were set apart for service.

In time, those men passed on their priestly ministry through a sacramental rite: the laying on of hands (see Acts 6:6). The apostles ritually placed their hands upon the men who would be their coworkers and successors. By this rite of ordination, the apostles conferred the gift of priesthood on a new generation (see 2 Tm 1:6). And so it has passed through the millennia, to the priests who serve us today.

Through this action, those who are ordained receive the Spirit of Jesus Christ, and so they receive power to perform actions that are properly divine.

So close is their communion with Jesus that they represent him—they *re-present* him. When St. Paul forgave sins, he said that he did it *en prosopo Christou* (2 Cor 2:10). That Greek word, *prosopo,* is very rich. It literally means "face." It can also mean "person" or "presence." In English, too, these words and their close relatives have overlapping meanings. If I am *present,* I am here *in person.* My *persona* is another word for the *face* I show you.

The Latin Bible rendered that phrase as *in persona Christi*. Thus tradition has always read it: *in the person of Christ*. (See, for example, the *Catechism of the Catholic Church*, pp. 1142, 1348, 1548, 1563, 1566, and 1591.)

That's how St. Paul understood his priesthood, and that's how we understand it today: to be the presence, the person, and the face of Christ the High Priest. By the sacrament of holy orders, a man is conformed to Christ in a unique way, a permanent way, empowered to do what only Christ has the right and the power to do. Thus, Catholic tradition refers to a priest as *alter Christus*—another Christ. In the words of St. Ignatius of Antioch (a contemporary of the apostles), by holy orders a man becomes, as Christ, the living image of God the Father (see CCC 1549, Jn 14:9, Col 1:15). So we do not hesitate to address him as "Father."

This is a privilege, yes, but it cannot be merited. It is a gift from God, and it is a ministry, a service to the Church. God gives it so that the priest can build up the holiness of Christians by dispensing grace from the very hands of Christ—through the sacred waters of baptism, the living bread of the Eucharist, and the holy oils of anointing.

Workers for Higher

The Catholic Church orders the ranks of the clergy in a *hierarchy*. Now, if we want to understand what that word really means, we have to unlearn some of its common uses. When we speak of hierarchy in a business, perhaps it evokes the "corporate ladder," where executives claw their way to the top, standing on the backs of their underlings. When we speak of hierarchy in politics, the picture's not much prettier. We imagine the "political machine," run by all-powerful bosses, a machine that grinds up candidates before spitting them out.

Unfortunately, those images sometimes carry over when we consider the Church's hierarchy. When this happens, we understand ministry as management—management according to a corporate or political model. At some level, we expect it to be a meritocracy, where power goes to the super-smart, and maybe that's what we want it to be.

That, however, is not how hierarchy works in the realm of the spirit. The word itself is derived from two Greek words meaning "sacred order." This order is indeed a pyramid, but—unlike the corporate or political organization charts—the pyramid is upside-down. Those who have received greater spiritual gifts must serve those who have lesser gifts. Jesus told his apostles, the very first ordination class: "If any one would be first, he must be last of all and servant of all" (Mk 9:35).

Yes, the priest is conformed in a special way to Christ, the Son of God; but Christ emptied himself, humbled himself, and "took the form of a servant" (Phil 2:7). So priests are ministers because they are Christ to the world, and Christ is a minister, a servant. And so the principle works, all the way through the Church's hierarchy. Bishops must serve their priests as well as the laity. The pope must live up to his honorific title: "Servant of the Servants of God."

As I said before: A priest is someone who mediates between man and God. A priest is someone who offers sacrifice. We learn in the Letter to the Hebrews that Jesus himself was the perfect sacrifice, offered "once for all" (Heb 10:10); but it is through the hands of his New Covenant priests that his unique sacrifice reaches "all," by way of the sacraments. We learn in St. Paul's First Letter to Timothy that there is "one mediator between God and men, the man Christ Jesus" (1 Tm 2:5); but we learn in the same chapter that we are to share in his mediation by interceding for "all men" (2 Tm 2:1).

A Priest Forever

When a man receives the sacrament of holy orders, he is changed forever. The sacrament confers a permanent character, just as baptism does. Once you are baptized, you are changed forever. You are a Christian forever. As the saying goes: Once a Catholic, always a Catholic. You may, at times, be an immoral Christian or even a lapsed Christian. You are, however, always a Christian. Baptism's character is permanent.

In the same way, once a man is ordained, he is "a priest forever" (Ps 110:4, Heb 7:21). He may be an immoral priest or even, if the Church has disciplined him, a de-frocked priest who may no longer celebrate the sacraments or be called "Father." Still, he is a priest.

As I said before, sacramental power does not depend on worthiness. Christ is worthy. He is sinless, all-pure, and all-powerful, and it is he who acts in the person of the priest—through his voice, through his hands. This happens in spite of his weaknesses or even his sins. It has been this way since the first generation, when Jesus ordained both Peter and Judas. St. Augustine put it forcefully: When Peter baptizes, it is Christ who baptizes; when Judas baptizes, it is Christ who baptizes.

This should come to us as good news. It is hard for us to endure scandal. But let's face it: that's part of life on earth, and it will be until God gathers us home. No one is worthy to be conformed to Christ. No one is worthy of the service of God.

Who, after all, can do what Christ commanded when he said, "Do this in remembrance of me"? Who among us can perform the divine prodigies, the wonders, that take place when a priest anoints or absolves?

These actions are not just difficult. They're humanly impossible! Yet many are called to perform them, and they are called by God, who should know better. To do their work, priests receive the power of God, who can do all things. And they *can* do all things in him who strengthens them (see Phil 4:13).

3

SPIRITUAL PATERNITY

The Priest as Father

PRIESTHOOD AND FATHERHOOD: We've spoken of two vocations as if they are very closely related. In one sense, this combination goes against intuition. As Roman Catholics, we are accustomed to priests who promise to live celibate lives. They do not marry, or date, or seek the good things that belong properly to marriage. Except in the rare cases of widowers who have been ordained, we do not ordinarily associate the life of a priest with the life of a dad.

Yet, paradoxically, we do. We address our clergy as "Father," following a Christian custom that goes back to the time of the apostles. The custom is indeed ancient, but the relationship between priesthood and fatherhood goes back even further than that: It's positively prehistoric. The Bible makes the connection at the very dawn of creation—and Christian doctrine takes it back even further than that, to the very life of the Trinity.

So it's an important matter, and it merits our attention.

Let's begin our investigation at "the beginning," the creation of man as it appears in the first pages of Scripture.

Surely a Temple

When we turn to the opening chapters of the Book of Genesis, we see God creating man out of nothing, out of the dust of the earth, and breathing life into him. The Hebrew word for man or mankind is *Adam,* and so we have come to know our primal ancestor by that name. The narrative, implicitly and explicitly, sets man apart from the rest of creation; for Adam receives "the breath of life, and man became a living being" (Gn 2:7). The sacred author says this about no other creature. So *breath* here does not mean mere oxygen. Animals breathe, and so do plants, but they apparently did not receive what Adam received from God.

In the original language, the meaning may be clearer. For in Hebrew (as in Greek), the same words denote "breath" and "spirit." Adam is here receiving the Spirit of God. Thus, from the beginning, he receives communion with God's own life. He has the power to participate in that life, share in it—live it.

God told Adam how to live such a godly life on earth. He gave him "dominion" over all other creatures and commanded him to "be fruitful and multiply, and fill the earth and subdue it" (Gn 1:28). Then, "The Lord God took the man and put him in the garden of Eden to till it and keep it" (Gn 2:15; the Hebrew is more accurately rendered as "to serve it and guard it").

As the Book of Genesis describes these acts of creation, it employs the language of purpose. We learn not just what God does, but we also get a glimpse of why he does it. He places man in the garden for a reason: "to till and keep it." Sometimes he reveals his purpose in the form of a command, as he tells Adam to fill the garden and subdue it and to "be fruitful and multiply." In these purposes, we begin to discover the mystery of the man's design.

For Adam's duties add up to something. God made man, by creation and by calling, to be a provider, a protector, a progenitor, and a guardian. God made him to be a father.

That's the way biblical religion has always understood Adam's role. As Eve was "the mother of all the living" (Gn 3:20), so Adam was the father of the human race. The Scriptures take this fatherhood for granted. All men, we read, are "sons of Adam" (Sir 40:1; see also Tb 8:6 and Sir 33:10). Yet for ancient Israelites as for later Christians, Adam's paternity was not reducible to the transmission of his genetic material. Nor was it simply the sum of a handful of stereotypically masculine duties. It consisted of something more, something deeper. The Bible makes clear that Adam's fatherhood was, above all else, a priesthood.

Adam's mandate is nothing less than an ordination. He is in the garden to "till it and keep it"—serve and guard it. The Hebrew verbs for these two activities—*'abodah* and *shamar*—appear together elsewhere in the Books of Moses, the first five books of the Bible, only to describe the ministry of the priests and Levites in the holy place (see Nm 3:7–8; 8:26; 18:5–6). These literary clues (and others) suggest that God intended creation to be a royal temple built by a heavenly king and served by a priest who shares in certain divine prerogatives: a divinized creature who, through his holy work, is also a co-creator with God.

The Genesis of Sacrifice

In the act of creation, God made a *covenant* with the cosmos. In the ancient world, a covenant was a promise, sealed by a solemn oath, that created a sacred family bond between two formerly unrelated parties. Marriage was a covenant. Adoption was a covenant. National treaties, too, could be covenantal, making one nation the "child," and thus the responsibility, of another. The "father" nation would receive obedience and deference from the "child" nation.

A covenant was a ritual act, sealed by a deeply symbolic sacrifice and a meal. It could be renewed at intervals—say, on an anniversary—through a memorial re-enactment of the sacrifice. Every covenant came with consequences. *Blessings* came as a reward to those who were faithful to the terms of the oath. *Curses* were the punishment meted out for infidelity.

These sacrificial rituals were the work of priests, who could also bestow the blessings or pronounce the curses. But who were the priests in the earliest days of the human race? Remember, from our last chapter, that a priest is someone who offers sacrifice and serves as a mediator between God and man.

Throughout the Book of Genesis, all priesthood belonged to fathers, and they fulfilled this role within the family. It was Noah who built an altar and offered sacrifice (Gn 8:20) on behalf of his household. So did Abraham (Gn 12:8 and elsewhere). So did Jacob (Gn 28:18 and elsewhere).

They blessed their children (see, for example, Gn 27:28–30). Sometimes, too, they announced the bad news of the covenant curses (see Gn 9:25).

Adam's priesthood had been a simple matter. God created him and called him to give his *whole life* as a loving sacrifice. When tested, however, he failed. When tempted by the deceitful and murderous serpent (see Jn 8:44), he chose to disobey God and protect his hide rather than lay down his life to save his bride.

Through disobedience, pride, and cowardice, he renounced his priestly duties. He forfeited the all-encompassing priesthood that had been his privilege.

After Adam's failure, we find men exercising their priesthood in more ritualized and arduous ways: deliberately offering to God a portion of the fruits of their labor. Since they were now expelled from the garden sanctuary, they had to build their own holy places. They needed to carry out physically, and enact symbolically, what Adam had failed to do spiritually: to offer service and to guard the sanctuary against danger and defilement.

That was the primary work of the fathers throughout the period to which they gave their name: the *patriarchal* period—that is, the time of the fathers. As fathers, they were priests. They were mediators and ministers of sacrifice, custodians of the covenant with God. By means of their blessing, they passed their priesthood on to their first-born sons.

The Book of Genesis tells stories of battles, journeys, fiery and watery disasters, trickery, treachery, loyalty, and jealousy—but the plot really turns on the priestly actions of the fathers: their blessings and curses, their sacrifices and mediation.

Calf-Hearted

As the tribes of Israel endured slavery in Egypt, they allowed their ancestral customs to lapse. Many of the people dabbled in the idolatry of their taskmasters' religion. Once God freed them from their bondage, he appointed one clan, the family of Aaron, to serve the nation as priests. They were to be ordained for this purpose, and they were to wear priestly garb: "You shall gird them with girdles and bind caps on them; and the priesthood shall be theirs by a perpetual statute. Thus you shall ordain Aaron and his sons" (Ex 29:9).

To Aaron and his sons belonged a high priesthood, but within the families the fathers still fulfilled a priestly role, at least for a while. In time, however, these sons of Adam defrocked themselves as surely as their primal father had. As Adam had forfeited his priesthood through his mortal sin, so these sons of Adam, the family patriarchs, forfeited their own. When the people of Israel were wandering in the desert, they grew impatient with Moses and Aaron—and with God—and they turned back to the worship of an Egyptian idol. They said: "Up, make us gods, who shall go before us; as for this Moses, the man who brought us up out of the land of Egypt, we do not know what has become of him" (Ex 32:1). And the tribes of Israel worshiped their golden calf with orgiastic rites: "And they rose up early on the morrow, and offered burnt offerings and brought peace offerings; and the people sat down to eat and drink, and rose up to play" (Ex 32:6). As the ancient rabbis noted: What the forbidden fruit was for Adam, the golden calf was for Israel.

From that moment, God gave the priesthood to the only tribe that rose to punish the sin of idolatry, the sons of Levi (Ex 32:28–29), who went on to fulfill that role in Israel for a millennium and a half. The priesthood passed from generation to generation by inheritance. It was genetic, the patrimony of Levite males.

Nevertheless, in the Book of Judges, we see that the transition to an exclusive Levitical priesthood was bumpy. Once settled in the promised land, non-Levite families still preserved a domestic priesthood, passed on from father to son.

In chapter 17 we meet a man named Micah, who conse-crates his son a priest for the purpose of worship in the family's shrine. When a Levite appears at the family's home, however, Micah pleads with him: "Stay with me, and be to me a father and a priest" (Jgs 17:10). A chapter later, Micah's plea is echoed, almost verbatim, by the Danites as they invite the Levite to be the priest for their entire tribe: "Come with us, and be to us a father and a priest" (Jgs 18:19).

In this transitional period, we see something revealing: Even though priesthood is passing out of the primitive and universal father-son arrangement, it is still associated with fatherhood. A priest is always a spiritual father to the people he serves, whether or not he is their progenitor.

Beyond Biology

With the New Covenant came yet another "change in the priesthood" (Heb 7:12). As God's Son, Jesus restored the original, natural priesthood of Adam to all those who re-ceive, through baptism, new life in his new creation. Christians are a kingdom of priests (see Rv 1:6 and 1 Pt 2:5) in Christ, who is the new Adam (1 Cor 15:22, 45). Christ the new Adam fulfilled the role that the old Adam was created and called for—the role that the old Adam had failed to fulfill.

Yet Jesus also established an order of priests to serve his Church through sacramental ministry. As we saw in the last chapter, he established this priesthood for the stewardship of his mysteries, his sacraments. St. Paul, for example, saw himself as a mediator (2 Cor 5:18) and minister of sacrifice (Rom 15:15–16). He was a priest. Moreover, because he was a priest, he was a spiritual father. He tells the Corinthians: "For though you have countless guides in Christ, you do not have many fathers. For I became your father in Christ Jesus through the gospel" (1 Cor 4:15–16; see also 1 Thes 2:11). St. John demonstrates the same basic assumption as he addresses his congregations as "my children" (3 Jn 4) and "my little children" (1 Jn 2:1).

Acting in the person of Christ, the ordained priest is the image of God the Father. In the priest, we come to see fatherhood that goes beyond the biological dimension. In a mortal man, we encounter a priesthood whose offering is eternal.

For the priest's life is, as Adam's was intended to be, an act of total self-giving. That is the reason for his celibacy. It leaves him free for ministry, service to the Church.

Thus free, he can give himself entirely, holding nothing back, as the eternal Father gives his life to the Son. Thus free, he can return that love, again holding nothing back, as the Son returns his life in love to the Father. The life they share—and the life the priest is empowered to share with his people—is the Holy Spirit.

In the New Covenant, then, the priesthood itself has become a revelation of the Blessed Trinity, a revelation of heaven on earth.

This is even more than Adam was given at the beginning of creation. In the new Adam, the natural priesthood has been restored, but also perfected and elevated, through the ministry of a supernatural priesthood, which shares in Christ's sonship and so images God's fatherhood.

4

STANDING IN THE GAP

The Priest as Mediator

I WISH I COULD SAY that I learned about the job of a "mediator" by applying myself, early in life, to lessons from Scripture and the catechism. But that wouldn't be true. The first time I remember being aware of a "mediator" was in the early days of free agency in professional sports. A mediator was the guy who got called in when a star player and his team had reached an impasse in their contract negotiations. The relationship was strained, perhaps, and both sides needed a professional to act as go-between—part messenger, part translator, part lawyer, part judge.

A mediator is literally a "middleman"—a negotiator who

makes friends of two parties that have been alienated from each other. The mediator resolves their differences and puts an end to their hostility.

That's a pretty good place for us to begin our study of priestly mediators. For after the fall, humanity was estranged from God, and the relationship certainly required mediation. Even if you and I personally are not to blame for Adam's transgression, we're still "at fault." For mankind finds itself standing at a chasm, like the Grand Canyon, a gap, a breach that separates us from communion with God, the communion for which we were created.

God sometimes sent his angels as intermediaries and interlocutors. They revealed his law, for example (see Gal 3:19–20). But he also called forth mediators from among his people. He raised up prophets, kings, and priests—men who stood in the breach and prayed, sacrificed, and labored to repair it. They represented God to his people. They represented the people before God.

Pleading Hearts

Consider Abraham. By the time the Genesis narrative reaches the eighteenth chapter, the patriarch (then named Abram) has been antagonized by the men of Sodom, an immoral rabble. After he received three mysterious visitors—

clearly messengers from heaven—the Sodomites came out to rape them.

God revealed to Abram the divine plan to judge Sodom (Gen 18:17–21). Knowing that the city could not withstand God's justice, Abram actually pleaded on behalf of his antagonists! He asked God if he would "indeed destroy the righteous with the wicked? Suppose there are fifty righteous within the city" (Gen 18:23–24). He went on to bargain, first getting the Lord to agree to spare the city for the sake of fifty righteous citizens. "If I find at Sodom fifty righteous in the city, I will spare the whole place for their sake" (Gen 18:26). Not content with that success, Abraham negotiated God down to forty-five, and then forty, and then thirty, and then twenty, and finally ten. (Granted, Abraham couldn't find one, let alone ten, but he was nonetheless confident in his role as a negotiator.)

The gap between God and Sodom was certainly wide, but Abram, out of compassion, was willing to stand there as a mediator. Reading the Old Testament, we find many others who stepped up to the task of intercessory prayer and mediation. King David interceded to save Israel from God's wrath (see 1 Chr 21:16). Solomon the priest-king prayed on behalf of his entire kingdom (1 Kgs 8).

By far, however, the greatest mediator in the Old Testament was Moses. It was he who represented God by revealing the law to Israel. It was he who announced God's intentions to Pharaoh. It was he who, like Abraham before him, begged God's mercy when the people sinned most grievously. God had freed the Israelites from slavery by means of astonishing miracles—parting the Red Sea as the grand finale—and he had promised them residence in a land flowing with milk and honey. Nevertheless, they were ungrateful and impatient with the hardships of their new-found freedom. They lost interest in the God who had delivered them, and they fell to worshiping the idols of the Egyptians, the bull-god Apis, represented by a golden calf.

For this, they deserved to die, at least as much as the citizens of Sodom had deserved it. But Moses appealed to God on their behalf. In fact, he went so far as to present himself as a victim, to die in their place: "Moses returned to the Lord and said, 'Alas, this people have sinned a great sin; they have made for themselves gods of gold. But now, if thou wilt forgive their sin—and if not, blot me, I pray thee, out of thy book which thou hast written'" (Ex 32:31–32).

Moses himself spoke of his work as mediation, and as necessary because of the people's estrangement from God. "I stood between the Lord and you at that time, to declare to you the word of the Lord; for you were afraid because of the fire, and you did not go up into the mountain" (Dt 5:5).

Yet Moses was not alone. He probably thanked God for

legally providing a hereditary cadre of priests to serve as mediators before God, offering sacrifice and intercessory prayer, making atonement for the sins of the people (see, for example, Ex 29:36–37). The tribe of Levi would, moreover, be preachers and guides: "They shall teach Jacob thy ordinances, and Israel thy law; they shall put incense before thee, and whole burnt offering upon thy altar" (Dt 33:10).

Prophets and Losses

As we've seen, the Levites were priests and mediators, by law and by birthright. In the millennium after Moses, they often failed to live up to the honor. They enjoyed the prestige that went with the priesthood, but not always the hard work and sacrifice—and certainly not the demands on their moral purity. This is a constant theme in the writings of the prophets. Through the prophet Malachi, God exposes the priests as "cheats" (Mal 1:14), offering sickly and castoff animals in sacrifice. Isaiah complained that, in his day, "the priest and the prophet reel with strong drink, they are confused with wine, they stagger with strong drink; they err in vision, they stumble in giving judgment" (Is 28:7). Led by such delinquent mediators, the people strayed further from God and further into sin.

Nowhere is this decried as strongly as in the Book of the Prophet Hosea:

> *Yet let no one contend,*
> *and let none accuse,*
> *for with you is my contention, O priest.*
> *You shall stumble by day,*
> *the prophet also shall stumble with you by night;*
> *and I will destroy your mother.*
> *My people are destroyed for lack of knowledge;*
> *because you have rejected knowledge,*
> *I reject you from being a priest to me.*
> *And since you have forgotten the law of your God,*
> *I also will forget your children.*
> *The more they increased,*
> *the more they sinned against me;*
> *I will change their glory into shame.*
> *They feed on the sin of my people;*
> *they are greedy for their iniquity.*
> *And it shall be like people, like priest;*
> *I will punish them for their ways,*
> *and requite them for their deeds.*
>
> (Hos 4:4–9)

Who was to blame for the increasing estrangement of God's people? The Levites bore the brunt of the prophetic oracles. Israel's estrangement was due to a failure of the priesthood. It was also due to a failure of fatherhood. Through Isaiah, God made the connection: "Your first father sinned, and your mediators transgressed against me. Therefore I profaned the princes of the sanctuary" (Is 43:27–28). Like Adam before them, the priests failed and were defrocked, deprived of their office, and exiled from the land.

Still, God himself expressed a longing for reconciliation, for a mediator to arise and do what Abraham, Moses, and David had done. "And I sought for a man among them who should build up the wall and stand in the breach before me for the land, that I should not destroy it; but I found none" (Ez 22:30).

Surely many were called. The entire tribe of Levi possessed the priestly vocation as a birthright! Yet the breach remained when no mediator had the will or the courage to answer the call with his whole life. God "saw that there was no man and wondered that there was no one to intervene" (Is 59:16).

If God wanted a faithful mediator, he would have to send his Son.

Mass Mediator

The Greek word for mediator, *mesites,* appears six times in the New Testament. Twice it refers to Moses (Gal 3:19–20) and four times to Jesus (Heb 8:6, 9:15, 12:24; 1 Tm 2:5). Moses was the mediator *par excellence* of the Old Covenant. He stood in the gap between Israel and Yahweh. He delivered God's word to Israel in the Law, and he interceded on behalf of Israel before God. Great as he was, however, he foreshadowed something greater still—unimaginably greater.

Christ is a more perfect mediator because he unites in himself both humanity and divinity. He mediates and administers a more excellent covenant than did Moses and the priests of Israel, a covenant that brings the Father and the human family together through an eternal redemption from sin (Heb 9:11–14) and perpetual intercession in heaven (Heb 7:25).

As mediator, Jesus reconciled the world to the Father in the bonds of the New Covenant. The distance that, ever since Adam's sin, had separated man from God is now bridged by the incarnation. Since the Word became flesh, divinity and humanity have been forever united in God the Son. In this sense, the mediation of Christ is absolutely unique.

Nevertheless, the mediation of angels and saints is not ruled out, since union with Christ enables others to share in the saving work of Christ. He has especially empowered the clergy of the Church for this purpose. As priests and mediators, Paul and Apollos and Peter are "God's coworkers" (1 Cor 3:9).

Thus Paul instructs Timothy to pray for others during the liturgy. "First of all, then, I urge that supplications, prayers, intercessions, and thanksgivings be made for all men, for kings and all who are in high positions, that we may lead a quiet and peaceable life, godly and respectful in every way. This is good, and it is acceptable in the sight of God our Savior, who desires all men to be saved and to come to the knowledge of the truth" (1 Tm 1:4).

Timothy would serve as a mediator on behalf of all mankind, from kings to paupers. So far, the instruction is unremarkable; but then Paul adds an explanatory line that sometimes confuses his readers: "For there is one God, and there is one mediator between God and men, the man Christ Jesus, who gave himself as a ransom for all" (1 Tm 2:5–6).

Wait a minute. If there is one mediator, and it is Christ Jesus, what business does Timothy have making intercession on behalf of the world?

If we read these lines in the context of Paul's other correspondence, it falls perfectly into place. Timothy, like Paul before him, will act in the person of Christ (see 2 Cor 2:10). As he immediately points out, this is the very reason for his ordination: "For this I was appointed a preacher and apostle (I am telling the truth, I am not lying), a teacher of the Gentiles in faith and truth" (1 Tm 2:7). Paul was an apostle. He was a presider at the liturgy. He was a mediator. He was a priest. And so would Timothy be.

Closing the Gap

With Christ came "a change in the priesthood" (Heb 7:12), and it's a change for the better. Jesus "is the mediator of a new covenant, so that those who are called may receive the promised eternal inheritance"; he has redeemed us as well "from the transgressions under the first covenant" (Heb 9:15). Since he is God, and since he has assumed our humanity into heaven with his own flesh, "he is able for all time to save those who draw near to God through him, since he always lives to make intercession for them" (Heb 7:25).

If he has ascended to heaven, though, that presents us with a problem. He promised he would be with us "always, to the close of the age" (Mt 28:20). So where do we meet the mediator now? How exactly has he closed the gap? The

Letter to the Hebrews places Jesus' mediation in the midst of the Church's assembly. The medium is the Mass, where we receive "the sprinkled blood that speaks more graciously than the blood of Abel" and Jesus acts as "the mediator of a new covenant" (Heb 12:24).

The New Testament testifies to the power of this Mass mediation. Because "earnest prayer for him was made to God by the Church"—prayer of the sort Paul described to Timothy—Peter's "chains fell off his hands," "the iron gate . . . opened to them of its own accord and he was led out of the prison by an angel of God" (Acts 12:5–10).

Armed and Ready

In the days of the prophets, God looked down and "saw that there was no man . . . no one to intervene" (Is 59:16). That, of course, was not the end of the story. Isaiah goes on, at the end of the verse, to say: "Then his own arm brought him victory, and his righteousness upheld him."

The purest Spirit, God took flesh and assumed arms so that he could stretch those arms out in the gesture of a priest; and by those arms he achieved victory. He is our heavenly priest.

This does not mean, however, that we have no further need for earthly priests. Jesus said: "Think not that I have come to abolish the law and the prophets; I have come not to abolish them but to fulfill them" (Mt 5:17). There has been a *change* in the priesthood and a *change* in the law; but these have not been abolished.

In fact, following the pattern established in the Sermon on the Mount, we can be sure that God doesn't ask less now than he did in the days of Moses and Ezekiel, but rather more. Read all of chapter five of Matthew's Gospel, where Jesus says:

> Think not that I have come to abolish the law and the prophets; I have come not to abolish them but to fulfill them. For truly, I say to you, till heaven and earth pass away, not an iota, not a dot, will pass from the law until all is accomplished. . . . For I tell you, unless your righteousness exceeds that of the scribes and Pharisees, you will never enter the kingdom of heaven. You have heard that it was said to the men of old, "You shall not kill; and whoever kills shall be liable to judgment." But I say to you that every one who is angry with his brother shall be liable to judgment; whoever insults his brother shall be liable to the council, and whoever says, "You fool!" shall be liable to the hell of fire. (Mt 5:17–18, 20–22).

As in the days of Ezekiel, God looks upon the earth for men who will stand in the gap. As in the days of Isaiah, he looks for me who will intervene. In Christ he has already brought victory. He invites his priests, priests of the New Covenant, to share in that victory, to share in his singularly powerful mediation.

5

Born to Be Breadwinner

The Priest as Provider

There's some truth to the stereotype of the workaholic dad. For better and for worse, a man's identity is bound up in his work. Remember, Adam was created with a purpose: to work—to tend and guard the earth, to fill it and subdue it. To be a father is not simply to be a progenitor, but also to be a provider, a breadwinner.

If you don't believe me, check the phone book. Turn the pages and you'll see long columns of English names like Smith, Miller, Cooper, Baker, Shepherd, Fisher, Shoemaker, and Weaver. Then there are the common names from languages other than English: Zimmerman (German for "carpenter"), Guerrero (Spanish for "soldier"), Ferraro (Italian for "blacksmith"), Kaminski (Polish for "stoneworker"), and so on.

How did these words become surnames? Men were identified with their trades. Alexander the coppersmith became Alexander Coppersmith, which distinguished him from Alexander the bricklayer. Fathers taught their trades to their sons, and with the trade came the name, the identifier, the identity. The names remained even long after technology had rendered some of the trades obsolete.

We men are hardwired for work because we're created by God to be providers for our families. It is one of the ways we bear his image and likeness. As God's providence supplies the world, so our providence buys the groceries. For "what man of you, if his son asks him for bread, will give him a stone?" (Mt 7:9).

Manna the House

As every priest is a father in God's earthly household, so every priest is a provider, a breadwinner. A pastor needs to keep a roof over the parish church and keep that roof in reasonable repair. And when the old roof has sprung too many leaks that can't be plugged, he's the one who has to raise money for a new roof. That, however, is not his primary concern as breadwinner. True to Jesus' urging, the priest does "not labor"—at least not primarily—"for the food which perishes, but for the food which endures to eternal life" (Jn 6:27).

Priests are fathers because they give new life, divine life, through baptism; but their obligation does not end with the pouring of the water. They go on to nourish the life of their spiritual offspring through the Eucharist. They discipline their "children" through penance. They instruct through their preaching and teaching. In short, they raise their congregations to full Christian maturity as contributing members of God's household (Eph 2:19).

Father provides for the family by giving us "the bread which comes down from heaven, that a man may eat of it and not die" (Jn 6:50). As God's children, we "partake of the table of the Lord" (1 Cor 10:21) in the Eucharist, which Jesus instituted in the presence of his disciples "as they were at table eating" (Mk 14:18). That's how he makes a living. That's how he supports the household—a family full of children, like my own, who always seem to be hungry.

As the tribes of Israel sojourned in the desert, God provided their sustenance. Manna fell from heaven, and water poured forth from a rock. There was, in that blessed day, such a thing as a free lunch. Ever afterward, it seems, God's people longed to receive that kind of care. They flocked to Jesus when he multiplied loaves and fish for them—and they hardly let a day go by before they asked him for a repeat performance, reminding him: "Our fathers ate the manna in the wilderness; as it is written, 'He gave them bread from heaven to eat'" (Jn 6:31). Jesus pointed out to them: "Your fathers ate the manna in the wilderness, and they died" (Jn 6:49). He, however, was promising his people something greater than manna. Manna, like loaves and fish, merely filled their bellies. Jesus promised to fill their souls, and fulfill their souls, forever.

He promised them true and unstinting provision at table, from now until the heavenly banquet. He promised them—and he promises us—the perpetual gift of the Eucharist, the bread of life, and he empowered his priests to provide it in his name.

Human nature remains today the same as it ever was. So does human longing. In these millennia since Jesus' earthly ministry, the Church still prays the childlike prayer that he taught us. In the Our Father we say: "Give us this day our daily bread." God answers us through the ministry of his priests.

Absent Fathers

It's impossible to overstate the importance of these priestly fathers in God's family.

In the natural family, fathers certainly play an essential role. In the ancient world, a fatherless family was condemned to live in poverty and shame. Widows and orphans were considered the poorest of the poor.

In the modern world, an increasing body of data shows that children of fatherless homes are more prone to drug abuse, divorce, dysfunctional relationships, and (as ever) poverty. Most youth suicides are from fatherless homes, as are most high-school dropouts and most young people in prison and juvenile detention. The more things change, the more they stay the same.

I don't want to paint a picture that's unrelentingly bleak and hopeless. Yes, I know families who have triumphed over such circumstances. I know mothers who have, through heroic efforts, raised good and healthy children. I know children who have found father figures in teachers, clergymen, coaches, and neighbors and have grown up to be fine fathers themselves. These friends are an inspiration to me. Statistically, though, such cases are exceptional.

Natural families need fathers. A kid needs a dad. That should go without saying, but it has become politically incorrect to acknowledge that simple fact. The fact, however, remains. Yet, as essential as a father is to natural families, he is *still more* necessary in the supernatural family, the Church. For the Church receives its unity—it becomes a household and a family—by the power of the Eucharist. "Because there is one bread, we who are many are one body, for we all partake of the one bread" (1 Cor 10:17). Thus the Church needs the Mass, and only a priest can offer the Mass. Only a priest has been ordained for this purpose.

Moreover, *each individual Christian* needs the Mass. Remember what Jesus said: "Truly, truly, I say to you, unless you eat the flesh of the Son of man and drink his blood, you have no life in you" (Jn 6:53). Those are strong words: no Mass, no life in us.

And no priest, no Mass.

By God's design and God's grace, there is no greater provider, no greater breadwinner, than the most ordinary parish priest.

Table Manners

Most fathers who bring home the bacon are bringing it home for one table. A priest must bring provisions for two tables. The Second Vatican Council teaches us that, through the Mass, the Church "unceasingly receives and offers to the faithful the bread of life from the table both of God's word and of Christ's body."

By means of both tables a priest feeds the twofold spiritual hunger of his people.

This dual understanding of the "Bread of Life" goes back to the early Church. Far from undermining the Catholic doctrine of the Eucharist, it enriches our understanding. The Mass becomes the privileged place for the proclamation of the Scriptures, the graced moment for inspired preaching. I don't mean to say that every homily we hear will be a rhetorical masterpiece. But we can be sure, if we pray to the Holy Spirit, that the priest will deliver a message we need to hear.

Sometime he'll do this in spite of himself. God makes up for what Father lacks. The Almighty, after all, can give himself as simple bread. It's no trouble for him to send his Word by way of the simplest words, even when they're stammered out and stumbled over.

This is why the Church commands "all the clergy must hold fast to the Sacred Scriptures through diligent sacred reading and careful study." A man cannot bring home wages until he's earned them himself. A priest can't give what he doesn't first possess. Before he can bring home an abundant harvest in his homily, a priest must labor many hours in the fields of prayer, study, and interpretation.

In our time, the hunger for the Eucharist is as overwhelming as ever. Many people, however, have been hungry so long they no longer feel the pangs. They are starving for the Gospel and starving to know the Scriptures.

More than seven hundred years before Christ, the Prophet Amos delivered an oracle from the Lord: "Behold, the days are coming . . . when I will send a famine on the land; not a famine of bread, nor a thirst for water, but of hearing the words of the Lord. They shall wander from sea to sea, and from north to east; they shall run to and fro, to seek the word of the Lord, but they shall not find it" (Amos 8:11–12).

Sound familiar? Who will feed those souls? As we mentioned in the last chapter, God looks for a man who will stand in the breach. He looks for a mediator, a heroic father, a true provider.

Keeping Body and Soul Together

A priest is concerned for his parishioners' spiritual welfare primarily, but not exclusively. A human being is a composite of body and soul, which will rise together on the last day. What happens to the body profoundly affects the state of the soul. The state of the soul certainly exercises influence over the body.

Thus a priest must never be indifferent to his parishioners' material welfare. He must provide for their spiritual needs but also help materially when possible—or at least help them to help themselves. "If a brother or sister is ill-clad and in lack of daily food, and one of you says to them, 'Go in peace, be warmed and filled,' without giving them the things needed for the body, what does it profit?" (Jas 2:15–16). "And whoever gives to one of these little ones even a cup of cold water because he is a disciple, truly, I say to you, he shall not lose his reward" (Mt 10:42). A priest learns these principles as he provides for the table of the word.

Throughout history, priests have been inspired by the lot of their parishioners to found great works of charity and mercy. The institution we know as the hospital arose out of Christian culture, founded by clergy. In the fourth century, St. Basil the Great instituted such a vast complex for care of the sick and the dying, refugees and travelers, that the grounds came to be called the "New City"! Closer to our own time, St. Damien, working alone, established humane living conditions for the lepers on Molokai. Countless priests have undergone medical, nutritional, and other training, just so that they could serve the needs of their flocks. Doing so, they follow a pattern of priestly self-giving that I have encountered quite often in my adult life. Anyone who reads history will find the same type emerging again and again. The role of the pastor, for two millennia, has been a fatherly role.

Priests are expected to share the lot of parishioners. I love the story of a third-century priest, St. Pionius, as he was undergoing the tortures that led up to his martyrdom. Some onlookers observed his condition with horror. Pionius didn't want them to think of his suffering as extraordinary, so he said: "You know what it is to suffer famine and death and other calamities." One of the bystanders acknowledged that Pionius knew the sufferings of the local people because "You went hungry with us."

That's what priests do. They share the lot of their spiritual children. When a priest is ordained, he promises to live simply. Some priests even take a vow of poverty; they resolve never to keep any possessions as their own. There are many good reasons for this; not the least of them is the natural bond it creates between the priest and the poorest families in his parish. A father cannot enjoy the good things of the earth as long as he knows his children are suffering for want of them.

Some historians believe that the High Middle Ages were brought low when so many of the best and brightest in the clergy died from the Black Plague. Why did so many of them die? Because they had willingly exposed themselves to the disease as they cared for their people and brought them the sacraments.

Love Is Like Oxygen

The priest is a provider, and what he provides is himself, body and soul. In the western Church, we see this self-giving signified in a powerful way by priestly celibacy, a more radical imitation of Christ.

Celibacy is not an end in itself. It empowers a priest to be a greater provider. Thus it is ordered to a greater charity, a greater love, a greater self-giving. A priest, like God, puts no bounds on his providence. Because he is celibate, he provides himself, holding nothing back. Pope Paul VI said that the priest's constant, undistracted, and undivided availability is a sign of his charity, which is drawn from God, and gives him "a limitless horizon" as it "deepens and gives breadth to his sense of responsibility." This is fatherhood taken to a degree otherwise impossible. It is a grace.

Have you ever flown on an airplane? If you have, then you know the standard lecture given by the flight attendant after you board. You're instructed on how to use the oxygen masks in case of an emergency; and parents are specifically told to attend to their own oxygen before tending to their children. Otherwise, parents might lose consciousness before they're able to help their kids. Most frequent fliers tune out the presentation; they know it by heart. But I'm often moved by that detail. The only way to get parents to put themselves first is by demonstrating that it's in their child's best interest.

Priests must take care of themselves. They must maintain a healthy diet. They must try to get adequate rest. They must study and pray. Doing so, they come to possess themselves more fully. They possess themselves because that's the only way they can give themselves away. And that's the only way they can provide for a large and needy family.

6

Go, Teach All Nations

The Priest as Teacher

I AM A TEACHER by training and by profession. I bear the telltale marks of chalk dust on my jackets. I'm one of those few grown-ups who mark their seasons by midterms and finals.

Teaching is what I've done through almost all my adult life. Even when I served as a Protestant minister, I considered myself a teacher, and my congregation considered me a teacher. When I preached, I taught. I imparted doctrine. I interpreted Scripture. I didn't have a doctorate at the time, but when a minister does hold a doctoral degree, it's customary to address him as "Dr. Billy Graham" (for example) or "Dr. John MacArthur." The word *doctor* (*rabbi* in Hebrew) is, after all, another word for teacher.

Protestants do not address their clergy as "Father." If you had asked me why, in 1981 or so, I would have referred you to Jesus' statement: "And call no man your father on earth, for you have one Father, who is in heaven" (Mt 23:9). I never stopped to consider that, in the previous line, Jesus had similarly proscribed the use of "Doctor" when he said, "you are not to be called teacher."

We have already seen that the apostles never ceased to use the term *father* or to speak of fatherhood, spiritual and biological. Presumably, they still called their dads by the same endearing name as they had before they met Jesus: *Father.* In this chapter, we'll see that they remained just as attached to the term *teacher.* For they knew that Jesus was not declaring a prohibition of terminology: He was establishing a new world order. "All authority in heaven and on earth" had been given to him, and so all existing authorities would now be subordinate to him, starting with those that are most important: father and teacher.

The roles go together, and they always have. Fathers teach. It's part of the job. We teach by means of word, example, and discipline—which is simply another way of saying "discipling." Schoolteachers, for their part, serve as father figures in the intellectual life of their students. In the ancient world, it was common for students, especially advanced students, to address their teachers as "Father."

Fathers are teachers, and teachers are fathers.

And so priests are both: fathers and teachers.

Tried and True

St. Paul called himself an apostle. As we've already seen, he spoke of his work as "priestly." He knew also that his office made him a teacher: "For this gospel I was appointed a preacher and apostle and teacher" (2 Tm 1:11; see also 1 Tm 2:7). In fact, he said repeatedly that a Christian clergyman should be an "apt teacher" (2 Tm 2:24; see also 1 Tm 3:2). Then as now, the Church needed "faithful men who will be able to teach others" (2 Tm 2:2), so that believers "may no longer be children, tossed to and fro and carried about with every wind of doctrine" (Eph 4:14). The Church's teachers, he made clear, were called, appointed, graced, and gifted by God himself (see 1 Cor 12:28 and Eph 4:11).

We Catholics say, with the great tradition, that our clergy holds "teaching authority." Priests are public representatives of the Church, and they have a sweet duty to teach as the Church teaches.

It's a responsibility they have received in an unbroken chain from the original apostles. One of the great heroes of the Church's second generation was St. Polycarp of Smyrna, who was a disciple of St. John the apostle. During a long life of ministry, Polycarp empowered others, too, to be teachers, not least of them St. Irenaeus of Lyons, one of history's most important theologians. As Polycarp was brought to the trial that preceded his martyrdom, the crowd of unbelievers identified him with two telling titles: "This is the teacher of Asia, the father of the Christians." Polycarp was a teacher and a father, and he was both because he was a priest.

Nor was St. Polycarp an exceptional case. Among the treasures of the Church are the "Acts" of the early martyrs. The earliest documents are often little more than court transcripts that had been bought from the Roman court stenographers. Their prose is as spare as anything you'll find in the novels of Ernest Hemingway. One of my favorite exchanges takes place during the interrogation of the priest St. Pionius, whom I mentioned in the last chapter. Once again, we find an early witness to classic Christian association of the priestly and teaching roles.

"I am a priest," said Pionius, "of the Catholic Church."

"Are you one of their teachers?" asked the proconsul.

"Yes," answered Pionius, "I was a teacher."

"You were a teacher of foolishness?" the proconsul asked.

"Of piety," was the answer.

"What sort of piety?" he asked.

He answered, "Piety towards God the Father who has made all things."

Teachers' Union

We call our priests "father" and "teacher" and even "mediator" even though we know from the Scriptures that we have *one* Father, *one* Teacher, and *one* Mediator. We can address our priests with such titles because they are our fathers in Christ, teachers in Christ, and mediators in Christ. Jesus empowered his clergy to act in his name—and in his person—when he breathed on them and gave them a share, a communion in his life (Jn 20:22).

At the Last Supper, he bade them to "do this"—offer the Eucharist—as he had done. That same evening, he also bade them to imitate his example of service: "You call me Teacher and Lord; and you are right, for so I am. If I then, your Lord and Teacher, have washed your feet, you also ought to wash one another's feet" (Jn 13:13–14). Thus he not only commissioned them as sacrificial priests and humble ministers; he also showed them how to teach by example. "For I have given you an example, that you also should do as I have done to you" (Jn 13:15). Later, as he ascended to heaven, Jesus commissioned them for the task of "teaching" all nations (Mt 28:19–20).

Our Lord embodied all the best methods of teaching. He taught by example and he taught with words of exhortation, correction, and instruction. He knew when to engage questions and when to rely on simple trust. He was a teacher of doctrine and a teacher of virtue.

From Pentecost onward, following Jesus' example, the apostles taught as grace enabled them to teach. In the Acts of the Apostles, we find them training others in basic prayer and worship. We find them delivering lessons in history. We find them guiding advanced disciples, like Apollos, still deeper in their knowledge of Christian theology and sacraments (see Acts 18:24–25). To make their points, the apostles are willing to be dramatic—to rend their garments and to strike the standard poses of orators. They've studied broadly in secular culture, and they're able to draw from popular poetry and philosophy. They refer to current events. They draw analogies and comparisons—to sports, family life, the trades, and the military—in order to make themselves understood. Most remarkably, they're able to range familiarly through all the Scriptures, calling witnesses from Israel's law, prophets, psalms, and chronicles. They were consummate teachers.

The best teachers we've known are those who are so passionate about their material that they'll go to great lengths to share it with us. They believe in their material. They believe it is important to our lives. Fathers, too, are passionate about what they teach, because the things they impart to their children are life's most important lessons.

The most impassioned teachers, and the most impassioned fathers, can sometimes seem brusque when they're teaching. But it's part of the fatherly teaching method. I've watched my children, one by one, learn to ride a bike; and I know that there is a point of frustration at which they would rather just quit. It's then that I've found myself speaking sternly to them, challenging them to concentrate, to reach farther, to stretch themselves, to push themselves. That's what a father does.

That's what Jesus did, and the apostles. It's what a priest must do, sometimes, for his spiritual children.

Eye Contact

Down the centuries, Christian art bears witness to the many ways believers choose to relate to their Savior. In frescoes, Jesus holds out a hand to heal, or to raise up Peter as he's sinking in the lake, or to pronounce a blessing. Some mosaics show him radiant in glory at the ascension.

Since ancient times, however, one of the most consistently popular works of devotional art is the image of Christ the Teacher. It appears on some of the earliest Christian burial caskets, and it's common in the Roman catacombs. In these early examples, our Lord appears with an open scroll, and his disciples surround him. In the classic icons of the Eastern Church, he appears alone, holding an open book (publishing technology had changed by then), and looking directly outward at—making "eye contact" with—the one who is praying before the icon. Sometimes he holds his free hand in the gesture of an orator.

What do these beloved images tell us? Christ is a teacher, and Christians love him for that. They gather around him in numbers, but they receive his teaching as if it's meant for each of them alone. He makes an effort to reach them in accustomed ways that are proven effective; he appears as an orator. And he draws them into the holy book.

It's good for a priest to study sacred icons. In fact, in the Eastern traditions, it is common to describe *the priest himself* as an icon of Christ. He is an icon of Christ blessing. He is an icon of Christ saving. And he is surely much beloved as an icon of Christ teaching.

A priest is not merely a sacramental functionary. Priesthood is not just a ceremonial role, and certainly not just an administrative role. Priests are teachers because they are conformed to Christ, and Christ is a teacher because he is the perfect image of the Father. And what do we know about fathers? One thing for sure is that they teach, and they teach with authority.

"And they were all amazed, so that they questioned among themselves, saying, 'What is this? A new teaching! With authority!'" (Mk 1:27).

Such authority should belong to fathers by nature, but nature is fallen and we have to study much and practice the skills we want to pass on to our children. This is true for spiritual fathers and natural fathers. When my son got active in Cub Scouts, I was chagrined to learn that I had to learn all sorts of new skills before I could pass them on to him, not the least of them baking a cake.

Priests must learn from the Master before they can teach like the Master—before they can teach as the Master. They must make time for study of the Scriptures. They must make time for deep and daily prayer. Again, no one can give away what he doesn't first possess. Prayer and study are not optional for spiritual fathers. (I honestly don't see how natural fathers get by without them!)

The greatest proof of a priest's authority is his exemplary life. By his life of total self-giving, a priest shows that charity is possible—even when it demands tremendous sacrifice—and that it leads to joy.

By his life a priest shows that people can be happy and fulfilled without possessions and status symbols.

By his life a priest shows that chastity is possible and continence need not be a burden. It brings a certain freedom.

What Henry Adams said of his teachers at Harvard is true a thousandfold of a parish priest: "A teacher affects eternity; he can never tell where his influence stops." A priest teaches the way a father teaches his children. He teaches them to teach. What a priest says from the pulpit, his congregation speaks to the world; and then the world becomes a better place for it.

7

LOVE IS A BATTLEFIELD

The Priest as Warrior

MY FRIEND Father Jim Farnan is a fighter. Please don't get me wrong. He's not a hothead or a brawler, but he is a warrior, as a priest should be.

Before he was ordained in 2000 he worked professionally as a bond trader and served in the United States Air Force. Both jobs prepared him well for the priesthood. He learned to negotiate, and he learned to follow orders. But nothing prepared him so well as his family's stories about a collateral ancestor, Father Lawrence Lynch.

Father Lynch was Jim Farnan's grandfather's cousin, and he died two full decades before Jim was born. Father Lynch died young. He was only thirty-nine, but he lived long enough to earn the name "Father Cyclone" and inspire a book about his life and heroic death.

Father Lynch was an Army chaplain in the Second World War. In April 1945, he was crouched in a foxhole on Iwo Jima with shells exploding all around him. A soldier nearby let out a cry. Father Lynch could see the man was mortally wounded, so he began to scramble out of the hole. His commanding officer ordered him to stay down, but Father Lynch rushed forward to give the man the last sacraments. As he held up the communion host, another shell exploded, this one tearing through the priest's helmet. The commander heard the blast and ran to catch Father Lynch as he fell. Gently he pried open the dead chaplain's fingers and forced them to place the sacrament on his own lips to prevent its desecration.

The commander lived to tell the story, as the chaplain's family told it during Jim Farnan's childhood, and as Father Jim tells it from the pulpit today.

It's the story of a priest and a warrior, and there are many more like it. Consider Maryknoll Father Vincent Capodanno, better known as "the Grunt Padre," because he worked among Marine infantrymen, foot soldiers who called themselves "grunts." Serving in Vietnam in 1967, he found his battalion suddenly outnumbered five to one. There were heavy casualties, and Father Vince himself was wounded twice, but he refused to be evacuated, saying, "I have work to do." Bullets flew, and he scrambled among the fallen, using his healthy arm to support his injured arm as he gave the dying men absolution or Holy Communion.

It caught up with him. He saw a man fall and rushed to his side, placing himself between the wounded man and the North Vietnamese gunner. When the gunner opened fire again, Father Vince was riddled with bullets. His men remembered him, of course, and they told the story of a warrior and a priest. In 2002 the Church opened his cause for canonization, and in 2006 he was declared "Servant of God," a step on the way to public recognition of sainthood.

Battle Acts

These priests died fighting the good fight. In their combat, however, they fired no weapons. Though bullets whizzed by and they were constantly in danger of bodily harm, the battle they fought was spiritual warfare. They had no enemies because their flock was catholic—that is, universal—and so it encompassed both sides in any battle.

Long before they entered the military, Fathers Lynch and

Capodanno were warriors. They were warriors because they were priests.

The military aspect of priesthood goes back to the very beginning. God commanded Adam to "guard" the garden sanctuary. He was to keep it from defilement—a task in which he failed, as he permitted the serpent to violate paradise.

In the period of the biblical patriarchs, the same fathers who functioned as priests also served as defenders of their families. Abraham waged war (see Gn 14:14–16).

When God gave the Law to Moses, he instructed Israel in military conquest and self-defense. The priests of the tribe of Levi, he said, were to play the most prominent role in any battle fought by the chosen people. They were to carry the Ark of the Covenant into the battlefield, and they were to attend the Lord's presence with trumpets and shouts. "And whenever the ark set out, Moses said, 'Arise, O Lord, and let thy enemies be scattered; and let them that hate thee flee before thee'" (Nm 10:35).

The most famous instance of priestly warfare is, of course, the Battle of Jericho. As Joshua pursued the conquest of the Promised Land, the tribes faced frightful odds and frightening enemies. Israel was outnumbered and inadequately armed, by the standards of conventional warfare. Yet they sought to take a strong walled city, whose occupants laughed at the seemingly pathetic challenge.

This is what God told Joshua, the army's commander: "You shall march around the city, all the men of war going around the city once. Thus shall you do for six days. And seven priests shall bear seven trumpets of rams' horns before the ark; and on the seventh day you shall march around the city seven times, the priests blowing the trumpets. And when they make a long blast with the ram's horn, as soon as you hear the sound of the trumpet, then all the people shall shout with a great shout; and the wall of the city will fall down flat, and the people shall go up every man straight before him" (Jos 6:3–5).

You know what? It worked. Ever after, this is how Israel fought its military campaigns, with the apparently defenseless priests figuring prominently in the narratives.

Priestly Investments

While we have grown accustomed to a strict separation of worship and warfare, the Old Testament makes no such distinctions. In fact, much of our religious vocabulary, even in the New Testament, is drawn from military life. For example, we call Jesus "Redeemer," and we think of this word as a theological term. Originally, however, it was used to describe the kinsman-redeemer (in Hebrew, *go'el*), the man sent by the clan or tribe to rescue a family member who had been captured or imprisoned by the enemy.

We also address Jesus as "Christ," that is, "Anointed One," from the Hebrew word *Moshiach*. Many Catholics today treat the word as if it is Jesus' surname. For believers in Israel in the first century, however, the title referred to the promised *deliverer,* whom many people believed would be a priest and many others believed would be a warrior-king. It turned out to be a man who fulfilled all those roles.

The prophet Isaiah had foretold such a Christ, priestly and fierce:

> *The Spirit of the Lord God is upon me,*
> *because the Lord has anointed me*
> *to bring good tidings to the afflicted . . .*
> *to proclaim liberty to the captives,*
> *and the opening of the prison to those who are bound;*
> *to proclaim the year of the Lord's favor,*
> *and the day of vengeance of our God . . .*
> *but you shall be called the priests of the Lord,*
> *men shall speak of you as the ministers of our God . . .*
> *I will greatly rejoice in the Lord . . .*

for he has clothed me with the garments of salvation,
he has covered me with the robe of righteousness.
    (Is 6:1–10)

Those "garments of salvation" were a military uniform, worn by the kinsman-redeemer, and the "robe of righteousness" was a priestly vestment, worn by the Levites. They complemented each other perfectly.

Jesus Christ is a priest, yes, but he is a warrior, too. He is a warrior because he is a priest. Like Fathers Lynch and Capodanno, he carried no conventional weapons during his earthly ministry; but he fiercely wielded the weapons of the spirit. His prayer in the Garden of Gethsemane is traditionally described as an "agony"—that is, a battle, a struggle.

Signing Up for Duty

The wars of the Israelites were real, historical events, but they also served as *signs* foreshadowing something far more momentous. Those bloody ancient battles were visible representations of the spiritual warfare that is always raging all around us. Our everyday struggle is no less real because it is spiritual rather than physical. In fact, our spiritual combat is more real, with still more grave consequences for more people. Indeed, it is the *primary* battle fought by those heroic battlefield chaplains and their brother priests who serve our parishes.

St. Paul put it plainly and in the most warlike terms:

> Put on the whole armor of God, that you may be able to stand against the wiles of the devil. For we are not contending against flesh and blood, but against the principalities, against the powers, against the world rulers of this present darkness, against the spiritual hosts of wickedness in the heavenly places. Therefore take the whole armor of God, that you may be able to withstand in the evil day, and having done all, to stand. Stand therefore, having girded your loins with truth, and having put on the breastplate of righteousness, and having shod your feet with the equipment of the gospel of peace; besides all these, taking the shield of faith, with which you can quench all the flaming darts of the evil one. And take the helmet of salvation, and the sword of the Spirit, which is the word of God. (Eph 6:11–17)

With our priests at the forefront, we are fighting nothing less than the enormity of evil, which rules "the world" around us and keeps it in darkness. We see the battle symbolically (but vividly) portrayed in the Book of Revelation, where St. John shows us monstrous beasts who snap their jaws at the most innocent prey: a pregnant woman, a baby boy. The beasts manipulate the world markets, spread sexual immorality, and grow strong from the immorality of the people they seduce; they get drunk on the "wine" of their victims' greed, fornication, and abusive power.

Who could stand against such an enemy, such a vast conspiracy? "The kings of the earth set themselves, and the rulers take counsel together, against the LORD and his anointed" (Ps 2:2).

We can, because "our help is in the name of the Lord, who made heaven and earth" (Ps 124:8). The Lord himself is our kinsman-redeemer. And he comes, with invincible sacramental power, shared out from the hands of our priests.

Todah Dedication

When in dire need or grave danger, the priests of ancient Israel would do a strange thing. Before offering a prayer of petition, they would thank God *in advance* for delivering his chosen people. The priests' action assumed that God would be victorious. They called this sacrifice the *Todah*— literally, the thank-offering. It was an offering of bread and wine. The rabbis predicted that, in the messianic age, all sacrifice would cease except the *Todah*. As the Jews migrated to other lands and translated their Scriptures, they found a fitting Greek equivalent for the word *Todah*. They rendered it as *Eucharistia*—the word the Church would apply to its great rite of thanksgiving, its great act of spiritual triumph and conquest: the Eucharist, the Holy Mass. At Mass, our priests lead us in giving thanks, because we already know how the war will end.

We see in the Acts of the Apostles that "many" of Jerusalem's priests—the men who had offered the *Todah* sacrifice—were among the first converts to Christianity (Acts 6:7). Lifelong warriors, they were quick to answer the call to arms, the call to service.

In times of peril, that's what good men do. They do it for home and family. Think about the tremendous surge in military enlistment after Pearl Harbor Day, December 7, 1941, and again after September 11, 2001, when Muslim terrorists attacked New York City and Washington, D.C. The men who signed up for duty were men who had something worth fighting for, something worth dying for—and so they had something worth living for. Many were called, and many answered.

What would have happened if the long-ago patriarchs had been unwilling to accept their fatherly duty to defend the family? The women would have been raped, and their children carried off. Their homes would have been laid to waste.

Can anyone doubt that today's parishes face comparable dangers?

Priests today must scramble through a battlefield, just as Fathers Lynch and Capodanno did, and the field is strewn with Christians who are spiritually dead (because of mortal sin) or spiritually dying (because of severe temptation).

Nevertheless, our priests, though they may appear vulnerable, are strong with the strength of God. They have power, in the sacraments, to raise the dead to new life and give new vigor to the weak and weary, Christians of flagging and sagging faith. When they raise their hands in blessing and absolution, and when they lift up the sacred Host, they give new life. So the soldiers of Christ can live to fight another day.

They say there are no atheists in foxholes. We can be sure that men in the trenches have a deep appreciation for their chaplains, and that it's no stretch for them to understand the ministry of the ancient priests who carried the Ark of the Covenant in battle. Years after World War II, yet another heroic chaplain, Father Joseph Ryan, recalled his first experience of battle: "I remember that first night. I had my gas mask and the Blessed Sacrament in the foxhole. Every young boy—we were all worried about dying—wanted to sleep next to the Blessed Sacrament."

If only we had eyes to see—if only we had spiritual sense—we would feel the need as intensely as those young men felt it. We would feel overwhelming gratitude to the men who answer the call and bear the Ark of the Lord in our midst.

8

ORDERS AND THE COURT

The Priest as Judge

S T. AUGUSTINE was not a man prone to complaining. For the most part, he enjoyed his work as a clergyman in the North African town of Hippo.

If he had one gripe, however, it was about the long hours he spent, every workday, presiding as legal magistrate in his town. Back in the fifth century, if you were the pastor of a parish or the bishop of a city, your people expected you to settle their disputes, address their complaints, and redress their wrongs. The early Christians took seriously the exhortation of St. Paul: "When one of you has a grievance against a brother, does he dare go to law before the unrighteous instead of the saints? Do you not know that the saints will judge the world? And if the world is to be judged by you, are you incompetent to try trivial cases? Do you not know that we are to judge angels? How much more, matters pertaining to this life! If then you have such cases, why do you lay them before those who are least esteemed by the Church?" (1 Cor 6:1–4). So, when they wanted justice, they turned to the Church rather than the courthouse.

Modern-day Catholics looking back across the centuries might worry whether this made for an overly "legalistic" approach to priestly ministry. Perhaps, in some rare cases, that may have been a problem; but "legalism" was surely the furthest thing from the minds of St. Augustine and St. Paul. Judgment and justice in the Church were not a matter of law enforcement so much as family discipline, and they naturally (and supernaturally) fell to the Church's fathers. Augustine accepted the responsibility, after protesting to no avail.

Augustine and his contemporaries were surely better off for his judicial handiwork. Nevertheless, we can be grateful that the Church, over time, has freed its clergy from such secular duties. Nowadays, a priest still presides as a judge in his parish. He still dispenses God's fatherly justice and mercy. But he does so in the confessional rather than the courtroom.

That is as it should be, and certainly as Jesus intended

when he bestowed an extraordinary power on his Apostles: the power to forgive sins.

The Gift That Keeps Forgiving

Forgiveness is not something human by nature or by right. When Jesus told the paralytic, "My son, your sins are forgiven," the Pharisees were shocked, and they had good reason to ask: "Why does this man speak thus? . . . Who can forgive sins but God alone?" (Mk 2:7). For sin is above all an offense against God, and so it can be truly absolved only by him.

What the Pharisees did *not* know is that Jesus is divine. He is God, and that's why he could forgive. It was his right to forgive. It belonged to his divine nature.

Yet he gave that authority—as a gift, a grace, a participation in divine life—to his apostles. "He breathed on them, and said to them, 'Receive the Holy Spirit. If you forgive the sins of any, they are forgiven; if you retain the sins of any, they are retained'" (Jn 20:22–23). On another occasion, he spelled out in more detail what that would mean: "Truly, I say to you, whatever you bind on earth shall be bound in heaven, and whatever you loose on earth shall be loosed in heaven" (Mt 18:18). How would the apostles know what to forgive or retain unless the sins had already been confessed?

Jesus' words, perhaps, are worn coin to us after two thousand years of frequent use; but we should often remind ourselves of their radical consequences. God himself was submitting himself, in perpetuity, to human authority. What humility! What a gift! A little over three centuries after Jesus spoke those words, St. John Chrysostom, a priest of Antioch in Syria, found them wondrous: "The chair of the priest stands in heaven, and he has the prerogative to administer heavenly things. Who has said this? The King of Heaven himself: 'Whatever you bind on earth shall be bound in heaven.' What is there that can be compared with this honor? Heaven derives the principal power of judgment from earth. For the judge sits upon earth, the Lord follows his servant, and whatever the latter has judged here below, he ratifies in heaven."

The apostles understood the import of Jesus' words, and we see them exercising their prerogative as judges throughout their ministry. They urged their congregations to find mercy in the discipline of sacramental confession. St. John said: "If we confess our sins, [God] is faithful and just, and will forgive our sins and cleanse us from all unrighteousness" (1 Jn 1:9). St. Paul made the further clarification that "confession" is something you do "with your mouth," not just with your heart and mind (Rom 10:10). Christians confessed their sins, audibly, to their clergymen. Otherwise, the apostles could not know what to bind or loose.

In most cases, the sinner's act of repentance was discipline enough. Sometimes, however, the apostles had to impose punishments and penitential acts. In incorrigible or scandalous cases, they even resorted to excommunication (see 1 Cor 5:1–5).

One thing's for sure: They were confident in their authority, as it had come from the Master himself. "What do you wish? Shall I come to you with a rod, or with love in a spirit of gentleness?" (1 Cor 4:21).

Elder Statesman

The authority of the clergy was judicial, dispensing justice and mercy; but it was also medical, for the sake of healing, wholeness, and the restoration of broken relationships. St. James wrote in his epistle: "Is any among you sick? Let him call for the elders of the Church." Now, remember, the Greek word translated as "elder" is *presbuteros,* from which we get "priests." He continues: "and let them pray over [the sick person], anointing him with oil in the name of the Lord; and the prayer of faith will save the sick man, and the Lord will raise him up; and if he has committed sins, he will be forgiven. Therefore confess your sins to one another, and pray for one another, that you may be healed" (Jas 5:14–16).

James is clearly setting the practice of confession in connection with the priest's healing ministry. Otherwise, he would not have used the word "therefore." Because priests are healers, we call upon them to anoint our bodies when we are ill; and, therefore, even more eagerly, we go to them for the healing sacrament of forgiveness when our souls are sick with sin. Because they are judges, they have the heavenly authority to forgive—the authority Jesus gave to the Twelve, and the Twelve passed on to the "presbyters."

Note that St. James did not exhort his congregation to confess their sins to Jesus alone; nor did he tell them to confess their sins silently, in their hearts. He instructed them to confess their sins aloud to "another," and specifically to a priest.

Like all judicial actions, sacramental forgiveness aims at restoring a relationship. In the courtroom, each case concerns a breach with society through negligence or criminal activity. In the confessional, it's all concerned with sin against God and neighbor—and a wounded or broken relationship with the Church. St. Paul said: "We implore you in Christ's name: Be reconciled to God!" (2 Cor 5:20).

Plane Sense

When Christians are regular about confession, it makes for a more peaceful "society" in the parish and in the Church. When the Church is at peace, it serves as a leaven of peace in the land.

Once I had the privilege of watching this happen—in almost perfect laboratory conditions.

I was delayed, along with dozens of other commuters, at a gate in the Philadelphia airport. Outside, rain fell in sheets and buckets, and there was no sign of a letup. Clouds were thick, dark, and ominous. The wind was hard against the windowpanes. The airline hadn't canceled our flight but had postponed takeoff once more. Apparently some flights were still taking off. So there was hope, but it was dim, slim to none.

In rows we sat with moods as gray as the day, contemplating the many appointments we were already missing and the many more we were likely to miss. We weren't talking with one another, really, except for the occasional grunt about the weather or, pathetically, the airline. Each of us seethed alone. I missed my family. I would probably miss my late-afternoon class. I would certainly miss my weekly appointment with my confessor.

As I forced my eyes away from the rage-inducing

window, they caught on something several rows away: a man in black pants and black shirt with . . . yes! . . . the telltale Roman collar.

It was a priest! At least I need not miss my confession. He could save some part of a day I had rued.

I worked up a smile, stood up, and strode past my fellow grumblers to approach the man.

"Excuse me," I said, "are you a Catholic priest?"

He was indeed.

"Would you hear my confession?"

He beamed. He would indeed.

So we walked together to an unoccupied part of the waiting area. We sat down. I confessed in a whisper, and he absolved me in a whisper.

I thanked him, and as I walked away, a man stopped me and asked: "Did he just hear your confession?"

I said yes, and the man scooted over to father.

And then something amazing happened.

A line formed.

Maybe the prospect of flying in that storm had inspired frequent fliers to prepare for death. Maybe people just felt guilty about blaming the airline for the weather. Whatever the reason, the Catholics at the gate were, one by one, inspired to confess their sins.

Then something else amazing happened. Slowly at first,

with little conversations bubbling up here and there. But the mood changed. People were making one another laugh, taking out their wallets to show off pictures of their kids and grandkids.

Now, I can't prove that all that came of the Catholic minority going to confession, one by one. But I couldn't think of any other explanation.

When the courts are in good order, it makes for peaceful souls, and it makes for a peaceful society.

Law and Orders

Our priests have a grave obligation to help us prepare to come to the heavenly banquet—not only at the end of our lives, but at every Mass we attend. Before we can approach the table, we need to get washed up. Thus St. Paul urged his Corinthian congregation: "Let a man *examine himself,* and so eat of the bread and drink of the cup" (1 Cor 11:28). Paul wants us—no, God wants us—to come to terms with our sinfulness and make a clean confession. He goes on to say: "If we judged ourselves truly, we should not be judged. But when we are judged by the Lord, we are chastened so that we may not be condemned along with the world."

Law and order get a bad rap sometimes. But they really are a prerequisite for peace. We chafe at discipline, but life is better for us when we live and work and play in a disciplined manner. God makes it easy for us to live that way, because he gives us good confessors, who give us divine mercy merely for the asking.

Is it any wonder that that priest smiled when I approached him at the airport gate? He was living the life of a king. No, he was living better than any king in this world. St. John Chrysostom gloried in the privilege of being a confessor, and here's how he explained it:

> Priesthood, you see, is more exalted than kingship itself, and its responsibilities greater. . . . If you want to see the difference between priest and king, examine the measure of authority given to each, and you will see the priest seated much higher than the king. I mean, even if the royal throne with the jewels attached to it and the gold encircling it strikes you as exalted, yet he has been chosen to administer the things of earth and has no authority beyond that, whereas the throne of priesthood is in heaven. . . . The priest has taken his place between God and human nature to bring honors down to us from there and take petitions from us up there, reconciling [God] to our common nature when he is angered, and rescuing us from his hands when we have given offense. Hence God even submits the royal

head itself to the hands of the priest to teach us that the one ruler is more important than the other, the less being blessed by the greater, after all.

To this I can testify as an eyewitness. If I were in court, I could, with good conscience, swear it on the Bible.

9

Restless Hearts

The Priest as Bridegroom

W E'VE GOT TO GET OURSELVES, once more, back to the Garden.

In this book, we've returned repeatedly to the story of creation, as we should in all our study of Scripture and theology. The Bible is not laid out chronologically. Genesis appears first not only because it speaks of the beginning of time, but also because it holds a certain primacy of importance. That compact story of creation is densely packed with theological truth. The early Christians called it the "First Gospel," because it foretells the coming of the Redeemer. It also provides the interpretive key for understanding human behavior, through all of history and till the end of time.

Saints since Augustine have pointed out that Genesis deals not so much with the "when" and "how" of creation as the "who" and "why." We can see in God's actions the reasons for our human drives and longings, our sadness and our satisfactions. Augustine put it well: "You have made us for yourself, O Lord, and our hearts are restless until they rest in you." That "making" is what we see in the story of Adam and Eve.

That's why you and I looked back to Genesis when we wanted to know the meaning of work, of fatherhood, and of priesthood. We found there that God built these things into the fabric of the universe and wove them into the fiber of our being.

There is, however, another great drive we have yet to examine: the drive to marriage.

What does marriage have to do with the vocation to priesthood? Everything—and Jesus himself made that clear. But let's not get ahead of ourselves. Let's begin at the beginning.

Priority Male

As God creates the universe, he evaluates its elements as they come from his hand. He makes earth and sky, light and darkness, birds and fish. "And God saw that it was good" (Gn 1:10, 12, 18, 21, 25).

In Genesis 2, the sacred author revisits the story, this time presenting it "close up." This time, we see the event a little more from the world's perspective—and the narrative presents us with something curious. As God is pronouncing his creation "good," he shocks us with the judgment that something in Eden is "not good." And we should be shocked. Remember, this is before the fall, before the Original Sin and its catastrophic effects.

After the creation of man, the Lord God says, "It is *not good* that the man should be alone," and then he adds, "I will make him a helper fit for him" (Gn 2:18).

He identifies the man's aloneness as an imperfection, an incompletion, a want, a lack, a need. It does, however, find fulfillment in the next divine action. He casts a sleep upon the man, takes out one of his ribs, and from it fashions a woman, Eve. Then the man says, "This at last is bone of my bones and flesh of my flesh" (Gn 2:23). Even in translation, the line rings not only with satisfaction, but with ecstasy.

In the fullness of time, Jesus himself returned to this story when he delivered the divine teaching on marriage. "Have you not read," he asked, "that he who made them from the beginning made them male and female, and said, 'For this reason a man shall leave his father and mother and be joined to his wife, and the two shall become one flesh'? So they are no longer two but one flesh" (Mt 19:4–6).

There we see it, from the hand of the creator and the word of the redeemer. God reveals our meaning and purpose through the construction of our bodies. He created us male and female, with significant and complementary differences between the two—so that each could, in a sense, complete the other. Pope John Paul II called this the "nuptial meaning of the body." Each of us, man and woman, has profound needs that the other can fulfill.

Again, this is *significant,* not merely important. It signifies something. The union of man and woman in marriage is an enduring and powerful sign of our vocation *to give ourselves* for the sake of another—to give ourselves to another. It will prove especially significant in our understanding of priesthood.

The Lonely Crowd

In our own day, the discussion is not so exalted. The body's nuptial meaning, in common discourse, is reduced to the sex drive, fulfilled, say the celebrity doctors, only if we have more sex or better sex. In this view, the two are not one, but merely "partners," as if they're striking a business deal or competing in a three-legged race.

Our society has (at least theoretically) made sex more available than ever before. Yet it has also returned its citizens, in epidemic numbers, to the state of aloneness, where things are "not good," not good at all.

What's wrong with this picture?

The problem is that sex, apart from that idea of self-gift, does not satisfy. In fact, it makes people feel more isolated and unfulfilled than ever—whether they're married or single. There's a Latin adage that has come down to us in many forms and is attributed to Aristotle: *Triste est omne animal post coitum—After intercourse, all animals are sad.* It can also be translated "all souls are sad." It is especially true of souls who have reduced themselves to an animal state, hoping to find human fulfillment.

The problem is that sex, apart from the idea of a sacrament, becomes a form of idolatry. The need becomes an implacable god that mocks the lonely and pitiable people who worship it.

The Christian tradition does not turn sex into a divinity or an end in itself. Christians view marriage as a sacrament, and so its one-flesh communion signifies a mystery still greater, still deeper. The Christian couple is thus liberated from the need to have sex be the final statement, the one true good, the only fulfillment of the only drive.

The momentary fulfillment of their embrace is itself temporal, temporary, intended to lead them to something eternal.

Groomed for Glory

It was St. Paul who first explicitly set out to decode the sacramental significance of marriage. In doing so, he drew upon the same story Jesus did, and even the same verse: "For this reason a man shall leave his father and mother and be joined to his wife, and the two shall become one flesh" (Eph 5:30). Then the apostle went a step further: "This mystery is a profound one, and I am saying that it refers to Christ and the Church" (Eph 5:32). The word *mystery* is the key, as in Greek it is *musterion,* which was translated into Latin as "sacramentum," and can be accurately rendered in English as "sacrament."

Marriage is a sign of the deep communion that exists between Christ and the Church. It is a relationship foreshadowed throughout the Old Testament, where the prophets often speak of God as the suitor or bridegroom of his chosen people, Israel. "For your Maker is your husband, the Lord of hosts is his name" (Is 54:5). The people, on the other hand, are portrayed as an unfaithful bride: adulterous, cast off, and even a prostitute.

Now, Christ has come as the bridegroom (see Mt 9:15), to establish a communion that is lasting and intimate. Like a loving husband, "Christ loved the church and gave himself up for her" (Eph 5:25). With this wedding, he has begun a new life, a new creation. The Book of Revelation depicts it in visionary terms as the "marriage supper of the Lamb" (Rv 19:7, 9), where the bride is the New Jerusalem (Rv 21:2). Indeed, it is in the Lamb's Supper, the Holy Mass, that the marriage is consummated and becomes a one-flesh union.

It is for this union that we were created. When we receive the Holy Eucharist, we begin the lasting, ecstatic union with God that we hope to know forever in heaven—the union for which we were made, and for which marriage is a sacramental sign. We have heaven already, though we cannot yet enjoy it with our physical senses (see 1 Jn 3:2; 1 Cor 13:12).

Nevertheless, the marriage supper has begun. The "end

times" arrived with the coming of Jesus Christ, the Word made Flesh. Heaven has established itself on earth.

Till Kingdom Come

The priest is a sign of that new world order. We mentioned earlier that he stands in the Church *en prosopo Christou*—as the person, the presence, and face of Christ. That's how St. Paul understood his priestly ministry, and how the Catholic Church has always understood the role of men ordained for ministry. The priest is configured to Christ in such a way that he can speak in his name, bless with his hands, consecrate with his voice. In the person of the priest, the bridegroom stands before his bride, and he gives himself and everything he has: body, blood, soul, and divinity. The priest stands as the bridegroom before the bride, and he stands as Christ, the eternal priest and the heavenly bridegroom.

Priestly celibacy is an outward sign, then, of Christ's total commitment to the Church. As Jesus' self-gift was total, undivided, and undistracted, so is the celibate priest's. He lives as the very image of Christ in relation to the Church at the consummation of history. "For in the resurrection they neither marry nor are given in marriage, but are like angels in heaven" (Mt 22:30). Thus, priests live now as all of us will live in the end. "Like angels in heaven," they have God; and so they have no need of marriage.

In the Old Covenant, the priests observed celibacy during their rotating terms of service (see Ex 19:15 and Dt 23:9–13). But Christ's term of service is forever. It is perpetual, as his priesthood is eternal.

Jesus' lifelong celibacy is a sign of that total commitment, and he described the celibate vocation as a grace, something "given" by God (Mt 19:11) "for the sake of the kingdom of heaven" (19:12), which is the Church on earth. "He who is able to receive this," he said, "let him receive it."

St. Paul lived that total commitment and likewise spoke of it in terms of the new age that had dawned in Christ. From Pentecost until the end of time is a time of transition and crisis. The apostle calls it "the present distress" (1 Cor 7:26). "Time is growing short," Paul says, and "the form of this world is passing away" (1 Cor 7: 29, 31).

From the moment of creation, God built marriage into the structure of the world. But now that very form is giving way; the signs are passing into the signified, images into reality.

The celibate priest bears witness to that fact.

In the long chapter on celibacy in his First Letter to the Corinthians, St. Paul gives other, practical reasons why being single is a good thing and should be desired. In fact, he wishes that *everyone* could have the gift (see 1 Cor 7:7–8). He points out that married men have "worldly troubles," "anxieties" about family and business, and not least the worry over "how to please his wife" (7:28, 32, 33). "The unmarried man is anxious about the affairs of the Lord, how to please the Lord" (7:32). He ends by saying celibate Christians will have the happier lot in life (7:40).

Fulfilled to Overflowing

As a married man who served in Christian ministry, I can add my own testimony to St. Paul's. In my role as pastor-husband-father, I found it difficult to balance all my obligations. I had to bear two sets of anxieties and, in a sense, serve two spouses: my wife and my congregation. It was hard for my wife as well. As Catholic converts, we are firm believers in the value—the theological and the practical—of priestly celibacy. In convert literature, there is no shortage of testimony from other former Protestant ministers.

I certainly don't mean to devalue marriage. I am blissfully happy with the vocation God has given me. In fact, it is my appreciation of marriage that enables me to appreciate celibacy.

In Hebrew, the same word serves to denote "wedding" and "holiness." The word *kiddushin* literally means "set apart." As one woman is set apart for marriage to one man, so the Temple's precious vessels were preserved only for liturgical use. The holy vessels could not be employed for a dinner banquet, no matter how great the guests.

Thus a priest is set apart for holy things, and he makes a holy sacrifice of the greatest gifts God has given him in the natural order. Remember the oracles of the prophet Malachi: It's a sin for a priest to put something second-rate on the altar. Thus, celibacy does not devalue marriage, but fixes its supremely high value.

For the sake of the kingdom, a man sacrifices the best of created goods—earthly marriage and progeny—and, as Jesus and St. Paul point out, he still gets the better portion.

What made me a bridegroom? It happened when I gave my bride my flesh and blood. And that gift became life-giving. When two became one, that unity was so real we had to give it a name. A priest has the power to be a supernatural bridegroom, bestowing Christ's flesh and blood with the life-giving power of the husband of the Church.

For the sake of that marriage, the priest forsakes any other marriage; and still he will be more fulfilled. For a man is not fulfilled when he is sexually active, but when he is a husband and father. Think back to the beginning. That's the meaning of our creation. That's the meaning of manhood. Holy Orders configures a man to be a husband and father in a far more fulfilling way—a husband to the bride of Christ, a father to many souls (see Mt 19:29).

That's why the early Christians understood celibacy as something intrinsically attractive. We saw it in St. Paul. We see it also in the Book of Revelation (14:4). It appears everywhere in the early Fathers of the Church. Around the year 150, St. Justin Martyr reported to the Emperor Antoninus Pius that "many" Christians were living the celibate life. Just a few years later, Athenagoras of Athens said the same thing to the Emperor Marcus Aurelius. Around the same time, the pagan physician Galen marveled at the manhood of Christian celibates. Through their "self-discipline and self-control," he said, they had become true philosophers. By the time of St. John Chrysostom (fourth century), celibates may have made up more than ten percent of the Christians in a large city like Antioch. In the later Byzantine

Empire, celibacy became so popular among the best and brightest that the government thought it necessary to impose restrictions on the monasteries!

Human nature hasn't changed since then. Nor has celibacy declined in its true value. Today, a re-paganized world is ripe to rediscover it.

10

Providential Paradox

The Priest as Celibate Father

R ETURN WITH ME for a moment to the time of
the biblical patriarchs—a time when a man's
worth was measured by the number of sons he
sired and the expanse of the lands he left to those sons. His
sons were his guarantee of security and defense in his old
age. To his sons the patriarch would pass on all that he himself had received in trust from his own father. To his sons,
especially the firstborn, the patriarch would pass on the
family priesthood.

Consider, then, the shame of a man who was childless, or
the woman who had borne no heirs for her otherwise prosperous husband. The Bible presents several stories of infer-

tile couples and their anguish, made far more painful by the ridicule of their neighbors, who called into question the husband's manhood and his wife's adequacy as a woman.

Consider the ordeal of Abram, who lived in the city of Ur in the land of the Chaldeans. Heir to a sizeable fortune, he looked forward with confidence to passing it on to many children. His very name, Abram, means "Exalted Father." Moreover, God himself confirmed him in his fondest hopes and called him to a still more prosperous patriarchy: "Go from your country and your kindred and your father's house to the land that I will show you. And I will make of you a great nation, and I will bless you, and make your name great, so that you will be a blessing . . . by you all the families of the earth shall bless themselves" (Gn 12:1–3).

With the divine guarantee, Abram went forward in faith and hope. We can be sure, though, that as he went—and as he advanced in age—the families of the earth were not yet blessing themselves by his name. Far from it, they were likely laughing up their sleeves at his very name: Exalted Father.

Yet God continued to make grand paternal promises, even as Abram and his wife Sarai passed seventy-five and approached a hundred years of age. At Canaan, the Lord said: "To your descendants I will give this land" (Gen 12:7).

Later the Lord added: "Look toward heaven, and number the stars, if you are able to number them. . . . So shall your descendants be" (Gen 15:5).

Numbering the Heirs

Could anything seem more ludicrous than the predicament of this childless man, far advanced in age, who bore the name Exalted Father? Is it any wonder that even his wife, Sarai, had to laugh at their prospects of progeny (Gen 18:12)?

As if this were not enough humiliation, God celebrated Abram's hundredth birthday by giving him a new name. No longer would he be called Exalted Father. No, even God agreed that the name was inadequate to the circumstances. Where most of us would round the name down, however, God rounded up. Way up.

"No longer shall your name be Abram," he said, "but your name shall be *Abraham*"—which means "father of a multitude of nations" (Gen 17:5).

I'm sure the new name didn't make life any easier for old Abraham as he made his way past the cruelest of his gossipy neighbors.

We know, of course, how the story ends. Abraham and

Sarah (also newly renamed) would bear a son, Isaac, who in turn would be father to Jacob, whose sons would bring forth the nation of Israel.

Still, God did not intend to bless *one nation* through Abraham, but a *multitude of nations*. God's original promise to Abraham was at the foundation of the message Moses took to Pharaoh, when he sought Israel's freedom from Egyptian slavery: "And you shall say to Pharaoh, 'Thus says the Lord, Israel is my first-born son'" (Ex 4:22). Israel was to be the first-born of many nations. Pharaoh didn't get it, but neither did ancient Israel. They repeatedly succumbed to nationalism and ethnic pride, preferring a strict separation from the remainder of the world.

More than a millennium later, however, St. Paul would note that the great promise came to Abraham not because of his covenant of circumcision—a rite he underwent at age ninety-nine. It came to him much earlier than that. So Abraham became a father to both Jews and Gentiles, not by a ritual act, but through faith. By his name "*all the families of the earth* shall bless themselves"—not just one family, the circumcised Israelites (and later their remnant, the Jews), but *all families*. (For St. Paul's discussion, see his Letter to the Galatians, chapter 3.)

All the families of nations, Jews as well as Gentiles, would come together in Christ. Thus the very first line of the New Testament identifies Jesus as the "son of Abraham" (Mt 1:1).

God made good on his promise. Abraham became the father of a multitude. All families of nations received God's blessing through his seed. His offspring was as numberless as the stars.

This is surely the story Jesus meant to evoke when he called his first priests to leave everything behind to follow him: "And every one who has left houses or brothers or sisters or father or mother or children or lands, for my name's sake, will receive a hundredfold, and inherit eternal life" (Mt 19:29).

Exalted Outcasts

The earliest Christians got the message, and responded, and they saw the tremendous rewards, even in the midst of persecutions. In the late third century, the historian Eusebius wrote something that's worth quoting at length:

> The reason that God-loving men of old had for begetting children is no longer cited because the begetting of children no longer has this meaning for us, since we can observe with our own eyes how, by the help of God, thousands of nations and peoples from cities,

lands, and fields come and gather through the evangelical teaching of our Redeemer, to attend together the divine instruction through the evangelical teaching. It is appropriate for the teachers and heralds of the true worship of God that they are now free of all the chains of earning a living and daily cares. Indeed, for these men it is now commanded to distance themselves resolutely from marriage so as to devote themselves to a more important matter. Now they are concerned with a holy and not a carnal begetting of descendants. And they have taken upon themselves the begetting, the God-pleasing education, and the daily care, not only of one or two children, but of an indeterminable number all at once.

In the eyes of the world, those ancient Christian priests appeared to be childless, aging without heirs; but they were not. Far from it, the priests of Jesus Christ, though celibate, would indeed be exalted fathers of multitudes.

The Lord had foretold this day, in marvelous detail, through the prophet Isaiah—again, worth quoting at length:

> Let not the foreigner who has joined himself
> to the Lord say,

"The Lord will surely separate me from his people";
and let not the eunuch say,
"Behold, I am a dry tree."
For thus says the Lord:
"To the eunuchs who keep my sabbaths,
who choose the things that please me
and hold fast my covenant,
I will give in my house and within my walls
a monument and a name
better than sons and daughters;
I will give them an everlasting name
which shall not be cut off.
"And the foreigners who join themselves to the LORD,
to minister to him, to love the name of the LORD,
and to be his servants,
every one who keeps the sabbath, and does not profane it,
and holds fast my covenant—
these I will bring to my holy mountain,
and make them joyful in my house of prayer;
their burnt offerings and their sacrifices
will be accepted on my altar;
for my house shall be called a house of prayer
for all peoples."

      (Is 56:3–7)

The Israelites considered Gentiles and eunuchs to be unclean, unworthy to stand in God's presence. Eunuchs were men who had been castrated, deprived of the exercise of their sexuality, so that they could be trusted to guard and serve a king's harem of wives. They were not quite men in the eyes of the world.

Yet Isaiah foresaw a day when *Gentile eunuchs* would stand on God's holy mountain, at his altar, and offer priestly sacrifice! Surely this is the day Jesus announced when he said: "There are eunuchs who have made themselves eunuchs for the sake of the kingdom of heaven" (Mt 19:12). Though the King of Kings has no harem, he loves his bride, and he now calls a new class of celibates to guard his bride, the Church.

Divine Fatherhood

Why did God name Abraham father of a multitude even before he had a son? He did not mean it to be ironic, but revelatory. God wanted to reveal his own fatherhood to the world by blessing all the nations, but first he had to purify our ideas of fatherhood. For we know fatherhood from experience: We have fathers. But human fatherhood is hardly divine. It works as an analogy, but all analogies are imperfect.

God's fatherhood is like human fatherhood, but more unlike it. Human paternity ordinarily requires several things: a body, male gender, sexual organs for sexual acts that are normally consummated in the context of marriage. Yet God has none of these: no body, no gender, no organs, no acts, no marriage. Nevertheless, he is the only real father.

What, then, is the purest essence of fatherhood? It's not primarily human and biological. It's divine and theological. It is, above all else, a spiritual reality.

Only spiritual beings can truly be fathers. Non-human animals cannot. They aren't persons who know and love. They have no rational soul.

Even among humans, the physical act of reproduction requires God's cooperation. Sexual intercourse, by itself, is metaphysically incapable of communicating the totality of human nature. When sperm and egg unite, they bring about the material substance for a physical body—but that body alone is not human. It requires a spiritual soul. That is what sets us apart from other animals. God alone creates each and every soul out of nothing. The creation of a person is a mystery of faith.

Ultimately, God alone is Father, and his perfect fatherhood is a spiritual act. Celibate priests are living and life-giving images of God the father, as they beget new children for the kingdom through baptism.

A priest, though he may not have his own biological children pulling on his sleeve, is not less a father than I am. He is more so, because he more perfectly resembles God in his fathering.

Sign of Contradiction

Abraham's contemporaries looked at him and believed he was cursed in his infertility. The early Christian clergy surely had to live with the same misunderstandings. Celibacy is always a "sign of contradiction" to a world given to disordered sensuality. That world finds no satisfaction in indulging its sensuality, but short of divine revelation people tend to arrive at that realization only late in life, after many mistakes and much pain. Many people indulge their sensuality to avoid loneliness, and they end up lonely anyway—a loneliness that's directly attributable to their self-indulgent lifestyle.

Celibacy is a mystery, but it's not as enigmatic or strange as its critics make it out to be. The Israelite priests observed it during their terms of service. Even today, secular society requires at least temporary celibacy of men who are doing the most important work. Soldiers go off to war, sometimes for years at a time, and we expect them to be faithful to their wives. Doctors must sometimes be separated from their spouses during part of their training; again, we expect them to be faithful. Even utility workers in some states are bound by law to leave home and family in times of emergency.

Sexual abstinence is a normal part of life for normal people. Married couples must observe it for several weeks after childbirth. In cases of illness, many couples must abstain for longer stretches and even many years. There is, as the Preacher said, "a time to embrace, and a time to refrain from embracing" (Eccl 3:5).

The sex drive is certainly a powerful force in human life, but it's not the totality of human life. It can seem to overwhelm us at times, but those times pass. Hours are long, but life is short; and what makes a life satisfying in the end is not sexual activity, but fidelity to God's will. For men, what makes life satisfying is fatherhood; and that, as we've seen, is not primarily biological, but theological.

Abraham knew it. The early Christians knew it. Every generation, though, must learn the lesson anew and teach it to an uncomprehending world. The priest teaches as he fathers, by his joyful celibate life.

11

FRATERNITY PLEDGED

The Priest as Brother

IT WAS MY PROVIDENTIAL PRIVILEGE to grow up in the shadow of an older brother. If imitation is the sincerest form of flattery, I spent much of my childhood sincerely flattering Fritz, who was far bigger than I, and worldly-wise, being three years my senior.

By imitating Fritz, I learned how to get ahead on the playing field—invaluable lessons for the smallest kid in the class. Watching Fritz, I learned how to do the things that pleased my mom and got us on her good side. Listening to Fritz, I learned to talk myself out of a jam. (I also learned how to get myself into a few jams—but that's a separate matter altogether!)

From Fritz, my brother, I learned how to throw and catch. I learned how and when to run. Most important, perhaps, I learned how to be a son. Instinct alone would have taken me a long way, but it was Fritz who showed me the shortcuts.

My childhood memories, I'm sure, have made it easier for me to appreciate the New Testament doctrine of Jesus as the "firstborn." St. Paul calls him "the firstborn among many brethren" (Rom 8:29), "the firstborn of all creation" (Col 1:15), and "the firstborn from the dead, that in everything he might be pre-eminent" (Col 1:18). Jesus appears as the firstborn in that great treatise on priesthood, the Epistle to the Hebrews (1:6), and the Book of Revelation (1:5). Hebrews even refers to the Church as the "Church of the firstborn" (12:23).

Reading the Old Testament, we learn that the firstborn son is the one who naturally receives his father's blessing, priesthood, and inheritance. He represents the father in a special way. He also represents the rest of the clan before the patriarch and before God. In the Book of Exodus, the firstborn is the object of both the blessing of mercy and the curse of the final plague. It is worth noting, too, that pages of the Old Testament are riddled with the names of firstborns who failed in their office—Cain, Ishmael, Esau, Reuben, and Manasseh, to name just a few.

In Jesus, however, God himself has taken flesh as the firstborn of creation, the firstborn of many siblings, the firstborn in a priestly family. This beloved Son—quite unlike my brother Fritz and me—is sinless and not at all inclined to sin. So he is eminently imitable. We imitate him to our own benefit. As we share in his life, we are better able to enjoy the life of the household. We bask in his attention and love.

Through holy orders, the Church's priests are conformed to Christ in a unique way. In our priestly family, they serve in the person and place of the divine firstborn, the only begotten Son of God. It is from him, above all others, that they learn to be priests. They succeed as they imitate him. They imitate him best, of course, as they spend more time with him and more time studying his words and actions.

Greater Works

Certainly one of the most poignant scenes in the Gospels is St. John's depiction of the ordination rite of the twelve apostles. Jesus employed the same ritual gesture that the Levites had used to prepare priests for service. He purified them symbolically by washing their feet (Jn 13:5–15; see also Ex 29:4, 30:17–21, 40:30–32). Jesus concluded the action by instructing them to imitate him, as brothers would mimic a firstborn: "For I have given you an example, that you also should do as I have done to you" (Jn 13:15).

St. John shows us that this took place in the context of the Last Supper, the meal at which Jesus modeled the liturgy of the Eucharist and instructed the Twelve to "do this" in his remembrance.

John, however, reveals more of Jesus' discourse on the occasion—an occasion quite unlike most other scenes in the Gospels. Here, Jesus acts not primarily for the benefit of "the world" he came to save, but for the sake of his priests. He says this explicitly in his prayer to the Father: "I am not praying for the world but for those whom you have given me, for they are yours" (Jn 13:9). Later, he acknowledges that, through the ministry of these men, God would bless many others, and so he adds: "I do not pray for these only, but also for those who believe in me through their word" (Jn 17:20).

The most startling part of the discourse, though, is certainly—for us as it must have been for the apostles—Jesus' promise that each of his chosen men would "do the works that I do; and greater works than these will he do" (Jn 14:12). Think about it from their perspective. They had seen him feed multitudes with just a few loaves. They had seen him raise people from the dead. They had seen him heal lepers and blind men and paralytics. Would he really empower them to do "greater works" than these? And what could those "greater works" be? Feeding bigger crowds? Raising entire cemeteries?

In fact, the New Testament contains no such record of the apostles performing works more spectacular than these in the material order. Was Jesus wrong, perhaps? Or are we misunderstanding the significance of the apostles' ordination ceremony?

No, Jesus was never wrong. The apostles would indeed perform greater works. They would perform baptism, which is a greater work than creation itself. They would forgive sins, which, as St. Augustine said, is a greater work than raising the dead. They would celebrate the Mass, which brings heaven into the midst of the world. These are divine actions. These are the greater works, and there are no greater works than these. It is for these, the sacraments, that Jesus ordained his priests.

Imitation, the Sincerest Form of Sacrifice

Priests participate in the life of Christ. Their communion is metaphysical. In this life, however, it is not complete; and the priest must strive to perfect that communion by an ever greater correspondence to God's grace, and ever greater imitation of Jesus' example.

One of the great lights of the early Church, St. Cyprian of Carthage, wrote extensively about the priesthood. Around A.D. 250, he wrote: "That priest truly functions in the place of Christ who imitates what Christ did, and consequently offers a true and complete sacrifice in the Church to God the Father."

How was the priest to accomplish this? Throughout his correspondence, St. Cyprian spelled out a program, down to the details. He said that his own life of prayer was "directed and guided" by Christ. He urged priests to "meditate on [the Scriptures] day and night and be careful to do everything that is written in them." He said that priests "ought not only teach but also learn, because he teaches better who daily grows and advances toward better things by learning." A priest's whole life was to be spent "imitating what Christ did and taught." Cyprian imitated Christ to the end, giving his life in martyrdom in A.D. 258.

In two thousand years, the program hasn't changed at all. A priest must pray, and he must study. He is duty-bound to imitate Christ in making a sacrifice of his entire life—whether he dies young or lives long to witness to a faithful old age.

The early martyrs were intensely aware of this. Around A.D. 107, St. Ignatius of Antioch wrote that he looked forward to the day of his ordeal, and he understood his own martyrdom in Eucharistic terms. He told the Roman Christians that he would be ground like wheat by the teeth of the lions; he would be poured out like a libation of wine.

St. Irenaeus of Sirmium, in A.D. 304, spoke similarly as he endured his final torments at the hands of torturers: "With my endurance I am even now offering sacrifice to my God to whom I have always offered sacrifice."

A priest offers his life as he offers the Mass. He does so in imitation of Christ. It was the Last Supper, after all—Jesus' priestly offering—that turned a routine execution into the sacrifice that saved the world.

Closing the Generation Gaps

A priest lives in the Church as a son, a brother, and a father—a son of God, brother of Christ, and father to his congregation. How can a man play all these roles in the same family?

In the modern scheme of things, it may seem unusual; but in the biblical world, the extended family lived together as a tribe, and young men (brothers) were expected to grow gradually into more fatherly roles. Thus, a grandfather, his son, and grandson might labor at the same trades—and all serve the household as domestic priests.

The Church took up this familial model. In Christ all

Christians are equals without distinction (see Gal 3:28)—that is, we are siblings. For Jesus himself was the firstborn of many brethren (Rom 8:29). A priest, however, is conformed to Christ in a special way; and so he looks up to Jesus the firstborn, but the priest himself also serves as a Christ, an anointed older brother, to his congregation.

St. Augustine saw no contradiction between his fatherly and brotherly roles. In his sermon on the day he was ordained, he told his congregation: "For you I am a bishop. With you I am a Christian." As a priest, he was their father. As a Christian, he was their brother.

In two thousand years, the program hasn't changed. It is our providential privilege to grow up in the shadow of such older brothers.

12

MYSTERY MAN

The Priesthood of the New Covenant

W E ALL DO WELL to follow the advice of the once-ubiquitous lapel button, and ask ourselves, "What Would Jesus Do?"

We do better, though, when we can first answer the question "What Did Jesus Do?"

In the last chapter we learned from St. Cyprian, a sage bishop of the early Church, about the importance of ongoing formation for priests. He would be horrified, however, if we put too clerical a point on his lesson. We should, both clergy and laity, desire to know and understand more about the priesthood of Jesus Christ and what it means for us who live in the Church—who live in Christ. For it is that priesthood—that offering, that sacrifice—that wins our salvation for us.

So, we ask: What *did* Jesus do? What *did* he do when he established the priesthood of the New Covenant in his blood?

What he did was no less than to recapitulate all of salvation history in his own life. You know what a post-game recap is, don't you? It's a summary treatment of the game's highlights, seen in light of the final score. The ending determines how we remember the drama and how we tell the story.

Thus the New Testament proclaims Jesus to be the Son of David, Israel's great king. Thus the Gospels present Jesus as fulfilling a role foreshadowed in Moses, going up the mountain to deliver a new law: the Sermon on the Mount. Thus St. Paul presents Jesus as fulfilling the promises God had made to Abraham. Thus St. Peter explains baptism by harking back to the story of the great flood.

It keeps going, too, all the way back. St. Paul explicitly presents Jesus as the new Adam—a first man who succeeds wherever his predecessor failed. Jesus succeeded as father, son, brother, warrior, teacher, mediator, spouse. In short, he succeeded as a priest; and in doing so he restored the natural priesthood to humanity.

This has tremendous consequences for every Christian.

For in baptism we have become a nation of priests. All of us have been called, in Christ, to do the work that Adam was made to do, but failed to do. Each of us is called to work as a priest who sanctifies the temporal order. Our altar is our desktop, our kitchen countertop, our laptop, our place in the assembly line, our diaper-changing table, our operating table. Our altar is the row we hoe. Through baptism, God has called us and empowered us to take the whole world and make it once again a sanctuary—and everything in it an offering. The priesthood of Adam has been restored in the New Adam, Jesus Christ, in whom we live and move and have our being.

The faithful sanctify the world through the common priesthood—but the Church's priests sanctify the faithful through the sacraments.

This, too, was foreshadowed in a powerful way in the Old Testament, in the person of a shadowy figure in the middle chapters of the Book of Genesis.

Shadow Play

Melchizedek is the first person in Scripture who is explicitly called a priest (in Hebrew, *kohen;* see Gn 14:18–20). In fact, he is the only person in Genesis identified as a priest of God

Most High, the same God worshipped by Abraham; the only other priests we encounter in that book of beginnings are servants of the pagan gods (see, for example, Gen 41:45, 50).

Melchizedek is called a priest, and in his brief appearance he does things we associate with priesthood. He blesses Abraham. He brings forth bread and wine as a covenant meal or thank-offering. He accepts a tithe from Abraham in tribute.

It is a curious episode, because Melchizedek, the proto-priest, emerges not from the chosen people, the clan of Abraham, but from the native population in the promised land. He is a Gentile. He is the priest-king of Salem.

In the subsequent books of the law, there is no such trafficking with Gentile priests. The only legitimate priesthood is the order established by God for the descendants of Aaron in the tribe of Levi. The only valid blessing comes at the hands of the Levites.

After this episode, we see no more of Melchizedek for a long time. The next time he is mentioned—and the only other time he is mentioned in the Old Testament—is in the Book of Psalms. There he is invoked just as David establishes Salem (now called Jeru-Salem) as capital of the kingdom of Israel. David names Melchizedek, who is both priest and king, as his predecessor; and David claims that this is the result of a divine decree: "The Lord has sworn and will not change his mind, 'You are a priest for ever after the order of Melchizedek'" (Ps 110:4). The statement is striking because, for well over a millennium, Israel had known only the Levitical priesthood.

David, then, is laying claim to a priesthood that is more primitive, more pure, a priesthood that predates the catastrophe of the golden calf, a priesthood that predates the order of Aaron and Levi. It is a priesthood that could serve both Israelites and Gentiles in a kingdom that is assimilationist—that includes both the chosen people and the nations of the world. Moreover, it is a priesthood that will remain with David's house, to be inherited by his son, King Solomon—but ultimately fulfilled in the anointed Son of David, the final priest-king: Jesus Christ.

David is announcing the impending restoration of the familial order of priesthood that had functioned for many centuries before the fathers were defrocked for their idolatry. Furthermore, he is announcing a new universalism symbolized by the priest-king Melchizedek, who was not a Levite, not even an Israelite, and not even a kinsman of Abraham.

David announces this with great fanfare in Psalm 110.

Then another curious thing happens. As suddenly as Melchizedek had appeared and disappeared in Genesis, so does he emerge from the shadows and immediately vanish again in the Psalms. Never again is he named in the Old Testament.

On Earth as in Heaven

Another thousand years will pass before Melchizedek steps again onto the stage in the drama of salvation history. Then, however, he is no longer a shadowy figure. Because salvation has come in its fullness in Jesus Christ, we know the end of the story, and we can see, in the Letter to the Hebrews, the full significance of the figure of Melchizedek.

In the Letter to the Hebrews, Melchizedek appears as a key figure in our understanding of the person and ministry of Jesus Christ. For the promise God had made to King David is now applied to Jesus: "You are a priest for ever after the order of Melchizedek" (Heb 7:17). What is implicit in David's claim is now explicit in the fullness of revelation: Christ "has become a priest, not according to a legal requirement concerning bodily descent but by the power of an indestructible life" (Heb 7:16).

Unlike the Levites who served in the Temple, Jesus' office

does not depend on law or genealogy (Heb 7:16). Nor is he bound by a term of service as the Levites were. Jesus the priest-king rules and ministers forever in the heavenly Jerusalem (Heb 12:22). The Levites could only copy the heavenly rites according to a pattern (Heb 8:5). Christ has "entered once for all into the Holy Place, taking not the blood of goats and calves but his own blood, thus securing an eternal redemption. For if the sprinkling of defiled persons with the blood of goats and bulls and with the ashes of a heifer sanctifies for the purification of the flesh, how much more shall the blood of Christ, who through the eternal Spirit offered himself without blemish to God, purify your conscience from dead works to serve the living God" (Heb 9:13–14).

The original form of the priesthood based in the natural order of the family is an earthly model of what has now been established in God's family. The Father has raised up his Son, Jesus Christ, as the firstborn, exalting him over the angels and over the Levites, the former mediators of the covenant. As the eldest son, he is the heir, given authority over all creation. He serves the family of believers as his brethren (see Heb 2:11) and his children (Heb 2:13).

In the heavenly Jerusalem, in the Church of the firstborn, Jesus offers the Father his body (Heb 10:10) and blood (Heb 9:12). On earth, through the Church's liturgy, we receive from his altar (Heb 13:10) the gifts he has offered. For us they have the sacramental appearance of bread and wine, the elements once offered in thanksgiving by the priest-king Melchizedek and later offered in the *Todah*, or thank-offering, by the priest-king David.

Everything old is new again—recapitulated, recapped—and now ever new!

Once a Father . . .

This is the priesthood that Jesus shares with his ministers in the Church on earth. The apostles knew this; and even though they were not from the tribe of Levi, the earliest histories tell us that they went about wearing the distinctive vestments of a priest. That would have been provocative, to say the least. But it was what they had to do. They were priests.

Their priesthood bore a permanent character, and they conferred that character upon subsequent generations through the sacrament of Holy Orders. Every priest is, like Jesus, "a priest forever."

The distinctive garb sets them apart when they're walking through a city, but that is just an outward sign of their inward grace. It is a sign of a life set apart, a life called out of the crowd, to find a heavenly fulfillment while still on earth. The collar of a priest signifies a manhood and a fatherhood that have been conformed to their divine and eternal models.

We've seen the difference, haven't we? We've seen it in the lives of Father Cyclone, the Grunt Padre, St. Irenaeus of Sirmium, St. Polycarp, St. Pionius, St. Damien of Molokai, and our quarterback, Joe Freedy.

God called these men forward to enjoy heavenly blessings, to serve in the priesthood of the firstborn. He called them to be men like Jesus Christ, fathers and older brothers to a multitude. He called them to perform greater works than Christ himself performed in his earthly ministry. And, one and all, they responded to the call with a resounding yes.

Many are called, like Melchizedek, from the shadows—from the obscure parts of society. They're called, as we've seen, out of the locker rooms and foxholes. They're called off the trading floor of the stock exchange. They're called from classrooms and boardrooms and even sickrooms.

They're called to be priests forever. They're called to something permanent—more permanent than marriage, which lasts only as long as both spouses are living. Priesthood is more permanent than the Pyramids of Giza and the Colosseum, more permanent, in fact, than the Himalayas. Long after the mountains are worn to dust, Peter and Paul, Ignatius and Cyprian, and your local pastor will still be priests.

This is the Christian faith. In the fourth century, St. Gregory Nazianzen wrote a famous oration mourning the death of his mentor, St. Basil the Great. He found consolation knowing that Basil, once a priest of the Church on earth, would be forever a priest in heaven. "And now he is in heaven, where, if I mistake not, he is offering sacrifices for us, and praying for the people, for though he has left us, he has not entirely left us."

Once a man has become a father, he is always thereafter a father. Once a man has become a priest, he is always fathering, always offering sacrifice for his people, never leaving them in his heart.

Do men always act the way they should, in accordance with the dignity of their vocation? Do priests? Do dads? Do I?

Sad to say, the answer is no. But still we owe them all, priests and fathers, a debt of gratitude. God has used them as channels of grace for us, and they have agreed to be used by God for our sake. Our natural fathers gave us food, clothing, shelter, and their hard-earned wages. Our priests give us the sacraments of Christ's love. Very few people will give us so much in life. Very few people, on the other hand, will render themselves so vulnerable to our scrutiny and our criticism. We need to learn to forgive them, our fathers and priests, and love them for who they are and what they've succeeded in doing. We need to stop judging them only by their failures. We should also learn to apologize to them, for our ingratitude at least, and pledge to love them better.

No man can, this side of heaven, truly live up to the gift of priesthood. It is too lavish a gift from too generous a God. When men know what the priesthood really is, they are instinctively attracted to it. It is intrinsically attractive. When a young man tells me he's never been attracted to the priestly life, I know one thing for certain: He's never really understood the priesthood.

Not long ago, the *Washington Post* interviewed a priest on the eve of his ordination. The young man said to the reporter:

> "There is a reason why they call a priest 'Father'—
> because you become a father of many. . . . You are with
> them when they baptize their children, when they bury
> their father, when a man and woman become husband
> and wife, to help them at 2 o'clock in the morning

when Grandma is dying in the hospital." His eyes welled with tears. "That's where the joy comes from, and I can't wait for that."

For him the joy and struggles of fatherhood have only begun. The struggles last a while, as I know from my limited experience. The joy never ends.

NOTES

CHAPTER 2

29 *"at the service of"*: Catechism of the Catholic Church, 1547, 1120.

29 *"must therefore be . . ."*: Ibid., 1551.

CHAPTER 5

68 *"unceasingly receives and offers to the faithful the bread of life . . ."*: Second Vatican Council, Dogmatic Constitution *Dei Verbum*, n. 21, November 18, 1965. Official translation at www.Vatican.va.

69 *"all the clergy must hold fast to the Sacred Scriptures . . ."*: Ibid., n. 25.

73 *"a limitless horizon . . ."*: Pope Paul VI, Encyclical Letter *Sacerdotalis Caelibatus*, n. 56, June 24, 1967. Official translation at www.Vatican.va.

CHAPTER 6

78 *the crowd of unbelievers identified him with two telling titles . . . : Martyrdom of Polycarp,* 12.2.

CHAPTER 7

95 *"I remember that first night . . .":* Quoted in David Scott, "A Centurion's Faith," originally published in *Catholic Heritage,* January–February 1992. Available online at www.DavidScottWritings.com.

CHAPTER 8

100 *"The chair of the priest stands in heaven . . .":* St. John Chrysostom, *Homilies on Isaiah* 5.1, quoted in Joseph Pohle and Arthur Preuss, *The Sacraments: A Dogmatic Treatise,* vol. III (St. Louis: Herder, 1920), 69. Language modernized slightly.

106 *"Priesthood, you see, is more exalted than kingship itself . . .":* Homilies on Isaiah 5.1, in *St. John Chrysostom: Homilies on the Old Testament: Homilies on Isaiah and Jeremiah,* translated by Robert C. Hill (Brookline, Mass.: Holy Cross Orthodox Press, 2007), 96–97.

CHAPTER 10

125 *"The reason that God-loving men of old had . . .":* Eusebius of Caesarea, *Demonstration of the Gospel* 1.9, quoted

in Stefan Heid, *Celibacy in the Early Church* (San Francisco: Ignatius Press, 2000), 119.

CHAPTER 11

137 *"That priest truly functions in the place of Christ . . ."*: St. Cyprian of Carthage, *Letters* 63.14.4, quoted in John D. Laurance, *"Priest" as Type of Christ: The Leader of the Eucharist in Salvation History According to Cyprian of Carthage* (New York: Peter Lang, 1984), 2.

137 *He said that his own life of prayer was . . .*: Ibid., 216.

137 *"meditate on [the Scriptures] day and night . . ."*: Ibid., 216.

137 *"ought not only teach but also learn . . ."*: Ibid., 216.

137 *"imitating what Christ did . . ."*: Ibid., 217.

139 *"For you I am a bishop . . ."*: St. Augustine, *Sermons* 340.1.

CHAPTER 12

149 *"And now he is in heaven . . ."*: St. Gregory Nazianzen, *Orations* 43.80.

ABOUT THE AUTHOR

SCOTT HAHN is a renowned biblical scholar and the best-selling author of a dozen books, including *Signs of Life, The Lamb's Supper,* and *Reasons to Believe.* He serves as the Chair of Biblical Theology and Liturgical Proclamation at Saint Vincent Seminary (Latrobe, Pennsylvania) and as professor of theology and scripture at the Franciscan University of Steubenville. An internationally renowned lecturer, Dr. Hahn is founder and president of the St. Paul Center for Biblical Theology and editor of the Center's academic journal, *Letter & Spirit.* His scholarly articles have appeared in various academic journals, including *The Journal of Biblical Literature, Catholic Biblical Quarterly,* and *Currents in Biblical Research.* A former Presbyterian minister and convert to Catholicism, Dr. Hahn lives with his wife, Kimberly, and their six children in Steubenville, Ohio.